CRISIS
OF SPIRIT

FIDGAL

First printing, June 2016

Crisis of Spirit/Fidgal-1ˢᵗ Edition
ISBN: 978-0-9950037-0-5

This book is dedicated to me for finally listening to the messages and to my lovely mother, Elisa Iuliano who gave me life and spent countless hours in the hospital and praying for a miracle which she received.
I love you dearly.

Also
May this book help many people (pre-angels)
to tell their own stories.

Kim,

May you lead with
the heart ♡
and follow
with the logic.

Peace
Maria &
Fidgal

Table of Contents

CHAPTER 3: CRISIS OF SPIRIT

CHAPTER 4: LIVING IN THE NOW

Chapter 5: The Universe

Chapter 6: Relationships

Chapter 7: Unconditional Love

List of Figures

PROLOGUE

MANY YEARS AFTER THE incident, I saw her coming down the escalator as I was folding men's sweaters at a local retail store. I said hello and she smiled and said hello back.

"Do you know me?" I asked.

"Yes, I do recall you," she said.

"You have been a school counselor for a long time, right?"

She smiled and said, "Yes, for over 30 years. I just retired this year."

"Wow, you have been a counselor for a long time, and you still remember me. Why is that?"

"Some people are hard to forget," she replied.

Finally able to let go of some of the grief I'd held for over 30 years, I simply said, "I know what you said to me."

She looked flushed, stammered some words and tripped over her feet while walking awkwardly backwards.

"I have to go," she mumbled. And away walked the woman who had hidden my story.

FOREWORD

THIS IS MY STORY. It involves characters that you might recognize from many different contexts: religious, academic and scientific. This story – which can certainly be defined as spiritual – had its start when I was five years old. I flat lined during a twelve hour heart surgery. In "actual" time I was "dead" for approximately 34 seconds, but the experience I had in heaven was timeless and profoundly affected my entire life since.

Throughout the experience there was Fidgal, my guardian angel who has remained with me since. I had encounters with other characters you will no doubt recognize who offered me guidance and wisdom, as well.

This book is organized into seven distinct chapters and contains the first twelve of the many teachings I received in heaven.

As you read this book, I encourage you to listen to the recommended songs. Music was a big part in both Jesus' and Einstein's life. They believed that music could change people's worlds. You can find all the songs either on YouTube or iTunes or Amazon. I feel that it is important to listen to the lyrics carefully, as sometimes the message is lost in the video images.

I often think in music. I live my daydreams in music,
I see my life in terms of music.
~ Albert Einstein

Over the years, my life stories have surfaced from flashbacks, from people telling me their stories, and from messages received in personal experiences. This book is designed for all learning styles. The visual figures are for people who learn visually, the "**Picture This**" examples are for practical learners and, of course, reading the book aloud is for audio learners. Anything underlined is very important in the chapter. For those who have heard some of this information before, this book will simply confirm what you already know. Other material in this book may be unfamiliar and difficult, at times, to believe.

From a logical side of thinking the term for human(s) is people, but in heaven they call us pre-angel(s). Throughout this book I refer to people as pre-angels. Pre-angels implies that we all are angels, not good or bad.

For those who are not familiar with spirituality, I hope this book will bring you introductory knowledge of what it is about and provide guidance to you in your everyday life. This book starts off as a human interest introduction storyline which will continue mid-section; then branches off to the 12 teachings. This book is based on a true story.

About Me

*"We limit our future from the things
that we cannot let go of from our past"
~ Fidgal*

HERE IS MY STORY …

Allow me to introduce myself: my name is Maria Iuliano and I was born to a loving family shortly after midnight on April 21, 1975 weighing in at four lbs. I guess you could say I wanted to be born on the 21st of April. I was born with three holes in my heart, a blue baby, and to add to the mix I was a baby who was not fully developed. I was so ill that I was airlifted from Sault Ste. Marie, Ontario to the Hospital for Sick Children in Toronto, Ontario at just one week old. They diagnosed me with congenital heart disease and I needed treatment.

At the age of one, I weighed in at eight pounds, and at the age of five I looked like a three-year-old. I was not eating much, which caused a lot of problems with gaining weight and growing.

At the age of five I went for a routine check-up and a test result showed that bacteria had developed in my bloodstream. I needed open heart surgery right away. Years later, my doctor explained that I had patent ductus arteriosus (PDA), meaning that one of the holes in my heart was not closing and blood was leaking into my lungs. I was drowning from the inside. I still remember taking the train to Toronto with my mother. My father stayed in Sault Ste. Marie, and was to come the day of the surgery. Unfortunately, due to serious health concerns I had the surgery one day early. They decided not to wait.

In the hospital, many doctors said that I looked like a three-year-old, while others said that I looked like a doll. I don't remember any of the prep before surgery or being wheeled in. I do remember my mother telling me years later that the doctors told her not to get too attached to me. My heart surgery was a complicated surgery, as they had to go through my upper back to get into certain areas of my heart. The surgery and recovery took approximately 12 hours. They repaired two larger holes in my heart and left a small one open. The small hole would close on its own as I grew older. I had many other small holes in my heart that were repaired as well.

During my heart surgery, I awoke to see myself lying on the operating table below. I felt like I was floating. I went back down to my body and sat right up. I looked at all the nurses and doctors that were working inside of me; no response showed when I looked at their faces. They all had serious, worried, or nervous gazes. At the end of the bed, I saw a man approaching with a gold and white aura surrounding him. He looked like an angel from a picture book that I recalled seeing at school. As he walked towards the foot of the bed, I noticed his tanned skin, peaceful appearance and white gown. He reached out his right hand and smiled at me. I rose from the bed, and he placed me on the ground. I looked up and started to walk beside him, then stopped and turned to see myself still lying on the bed. The doctors and nurses were moving quite quickly, and many pre-angels were coming in to assist them. I stood there with a sad face and looked up at the angel. He squatted down to my level and said, "Come with me. I will take you away from all this pain."

I continued to walk down a long stretched hospital hallway. At the end was an elevator, but we faded before we reached the elevator.

As we continued to walk I saw a bright, peaceful white light beaming in a cloudy tunnel. I felt relaxed and comfortable and safe, and there was no pain. I was in heaven. White clouds and a large gate stood before me. I looked up to see what seemed like a man with short thick brown hair, and beautiful bluish green eyes, tanned skin, and a beard standing at the gate. He said his name was Jesus. I recalled seeing his face on the cross at church. Jesus introduced three spirits at the gate. One was Mr. Albert Einstein. One was a woman who I figured out later that was my grandmother, whom I had never met. The third was one of the twelve disciples. Everything in heaven looked so new and fresh and young, and everyone I met had such nice, smooth, clear, healthy skin. Jesus told me that they were all at the same age as when he died on the cross, so around 32. I received the grand tour of heaven and met other spirits. Some, still to this day, I do not remember or recognize. I went to different dimensions and met beautiful angels. Though I spent a lot of time with various spirits there, in this book I will focus on the teachings that Jesus and Albert Einstein gave me.

I recall having cookie time with Jesus and walking in the amazing rain forest with Albert Einstein. I must say those different shaped cookies were so delicious and I never found them on earth. Jesus explained about love and our deep side (the right side of our brain). What an amazing, down to earth spirit Jesus was, and funny too. As for Albert Einstein, the first thing I noticed was that he had a bit of puffy white hair; it reminded me of when I wake up in the morning. He was an odd spirit, one who at times I couldn't figure out but he had patience with me. When I didn't understand something, I guess I would look at him strangely, and he smiled at me and explained it in a different way. He explained all about surviving using the logical side and that everything has energy. Both Jesus and Einstein were amazing mentors and gave me such profound messages. I loved heaven, the food, music, laughter, angels, and the amazing things that I saw. I felt at home, and I wanted to stay. All of a sudden, I heard rumbling and saw shaking in the clouds. There was a video underneath my feet, a vision of me lying on the table in the hospital and the doctors looking at the monitor and saying "Time of death" and then everything froze.

Jesus knelt on one knee and said "You must go back. You will return."

I shouted and cried and screamed, "I want to stay! I want to stay!"

Jesus patted my head and said, "Now, now. You can always come back anytime while you are healing down there."

He pointed to the angel who brought me to heaven and said he would be with me all the time while down there. He introduced him to me as Fidgal. Fidgal was standing near the front of the gate with a couple of pretty girl angels. He was laughing and smiling.

Jesus waved at him, "Fidgal you have been chosen to guide this glorious soul, and anytime she would like to come for a visit, you will bring her back to me."

Fidgal nodded his head and put out his hand. I continued to cry and then started kicking. Jesus was very concerned. Again he knelt down to my level and gave me a grand hug. He promised that I would come back later, and that if I closed my eyes and fell asleep Fidgal would bring me back. All I had to do was ask him. I told him there was too much pain down there and I wanted to stay in heaven. Jesus placed his hand on my chest and a beam of light shone through my heart illuminating the holes. He gave me a hug and I calmed down. I must say there is a lot of hugging in heaven and they give the best hugs. The monitor beeped, and the next thing I knew I was in the recovery room awake.

My mom stayed with me day and night. She had incredible energy and would always smile at me and send me positive thoughts and love. She basically lived at the hospital, even though she could have gone to Ronald McDonald housing. The nurses were pleasant to her; one nurse gave her a cot to sleep on next to me.

I very much loved the music in heaven and told the doctors and my mother that I liked the music during my surgery. I repeated this so much that my mother bought a small radio and placed it beside my bed. I would fall asleep to the music and astral travel (out-of-body experience) to heaven. What my mother and the doctors didn't know was that at night the music changed to heavenly music by Fidgal. Every morning when I woke up I heard the same song called Morning Train by

Sheena Easton playing. I think Fidgal liked that song and played it often. I loved to sleep, and the rest saved my life. Fidgal was excellent to me, and he would bring me back to heaven all hours of the day. I didn't just go to heaven; I went to various other places on earth too.

After almost a year, I healed from my heart surgery. I was on no medication and had no problems with my heart anymore. The doctors said it was a success and my parents were thrilled by the news. Many years later, I heard that what happened to me from a medical point of view was labeled "spontaneous remission (healing)" which happens when an unexpected improvement or cure of a disease occurs. I call it a miracle. The last time in heaven, as I was leaving, Jesus also explained that any time I needed assistance Fidgal would be there for me. I thanked him and the others and told them that I would miss them dearly, especially Jesus.

Shortly after, I returned to my hometown of Sault Ste. Marie, Ontario and went back to school. It was a Catholic school with a nun for a principal. I missed too much school, so had to repeat grade one again. I was so excited to be alive and talked to my classmates about my journey in heaven. I explained what I saw and at times my classmates gave me strange looks. I remember feeling goose bumps when I talked about heaven but felt sad at the same time because the children did not have the same fun, happy, reaction that I did. One day, the school counselor pulled me aside and wanted to know what I was talking to the classmates about, so I told her. She pointed her finger and said to never speak about heaven and angels again and if I did I would be taken away and end up in a different hospital. I had just returned from the hospital, and I love my parents. Although I didn't feel much pain during my time in the hospital as I was in heaven most of the time, I didn't like needles and all that other painful stuff. Jesus told me that I needed to complete my purpose and didn't say anything about returning to the hospital, so I knew this wasn't the same hospital that I was going to. I was frightened, in shock, and did not like this lady's energy or her tone of voice. The school counselor also came to my house a couple of times, to check up on me, so my mother said.

I was forced to suppress my feelings and knowledge. This was harsh for me to endure, so in class I would doodle and not pay attention to the teacher. I was obsessed with trying to keep those memories of heaven alive in my mind. I was so scared in school that my behavior changed and I withdrew from various activities and conversations. Years later, I learned that this experience was a crisis of spirit and it happened to me at the age of six years.

It didn't help that many times I went to the Hospital for Sick Children in Toronto for regular check-ups and missed a lot of school. At this time the principal, counselor, and psychologist decided to place me in a special education class. Even in that class I suppressed what I knew about heaven, although in special education I had more creative time to think and draw. I was mixed in with behavioral challenged students which sometimes made it difficult to learn because some students would just burst out loud. Fidgal convinced me to do better in the class and helped me with understanding the school work. He also explained that this would be an excellent opportunity to learn about behaviors and different teaching styles. The teachers there had more patience and better energy than the other teachers that I had.

Years went by and I still couldn't tell anyone about my heaven journey as I was too afraid of what would happen to me. I learned by watching strange movies that many pre-angels ended up in what was called the nut house, so I stayed in silence. Until now...

First I must give some information and then I will return to my story.

Song Reference:
I Will Rest in You **by Jaci Velasquez**

INTRODUCTION

"The key to not assuming is to define every word"
~ Fidgal

BOTH JESUS AND EINSTEIN convinced me at an early age of these teachings and of their explanation of living in this dimension. Being so young, with a limited vocabulary, at times I wasn't convinced about these teachings or couldn't quite understand them. Jesus explained everything in simple terms while Einstein explained things in complex terms and sometimes terms in strange sentence formats. It was difficult to remember this information, but with my angel Fidgal guiding me in writing this book, I feel confident that the teachings that I speak of and use in my daily life are profound. They taught me how to achieve balance using both the logical and deep side of existence.

Albert Einstein taught me about energy and the logical side; Jesus gave me information about the heart and the deep side of living. Both expressed their views, but one message that they told me at the beginning of my visit was particularly significant. While living on earth in this dimension there is a larger world that we do not see.

Where we are living today (earth) is the illusion. We believe it's real because it's tangible and we feel it, see it, taste it, and smell it, but if we peel off the layers we are just in the same world as before. Both gave me hidden messages that lie in our bodies, that to obtain peace and balance, we must lead with the heart. Our body is a magical creation that can heal itself from a deeper side and on earth it is always examined medically from a more logical point of view.

The universe is the source of creation and existence of all life. Pre-angels use different terms for the universe such as God, angels, higher power, source, to understand the existence of life. In this book, I will use the term "the universe" to represent the existence of life.

Jesus and Einstein explained that our minds are split into two halves: the deep side and the logical side. Einstein focused more on the logical side and explained that our left side of our mind is the logical side, where we store learned facts, aids to survival, facts about money, and the ego. The left side of our mind controls the right side of our body. Einstein was a very interesting character who I didn't care for at first as his sense of humor was at times over my head. He believed if a problem you have is giving you grief, step aside and do the opposite of what the problem is defined as. In other words, if the problem was logical, do a deep side exercise to break free from the logical mind thinking. For example, say you had a math problem to do. Take a break and do a deep sided therapy & exercise. When you return to the problem, the answer will appear easier.

Jesus taught me more about deep pre-angels and used various figures to explain them to me. He explained that the right side, which is known as the deep side of our mind, controls creativity, love, emotions, spirituality, and connects with our heart. The right side of our brain also controls the left side of our body, which is the heart. The heart is in the middle, but slightly to the left of our chest.

First, we need to master the concept of energy. Einstein explained that everything (pre-angels, items, entities) holds energy and has energy, which is negative or positive. This always existing energy, called "invisible vibrational energy", cannot be seen, but only felt with our intuition. It exists if we want to believe it or not. I am sure that you have had the experience where you meet someone and notice the energy that they project. It's the same concept. Vibration means the energy resonates, including in pre-angels and objects, even the food we eat. Einstein explained it like this. "You love your moms' chicken soup right? That's because of the 'meraki' she puts in it which makes you feel better. Meraki is putting your soul, passion, creativity, and love into what you are doing which can be translated also as putting positive invisible vibrational energy into your work. Chicken soup bought at a store does not give the same positive energy effects for us to get better."

Einstein used this word meraki often and I said it often too but when I was young I don't think I pronounced it correctly. As I recall, Einstein loved highly complex terms, so he had to explain his teachings to me many times.

CRISIS
OF SPIRIT

CHAPTER 1

Deep Pre-angels

"Those who understand to lead with the heart
will always be rewarded"
~ Fidgal

WE ARE SPIRITUAL BEINGS having a mortal experience. We come to a point in our lives when we want to understand our existence and need to be able to accept it to move on. Deep pre-angels are exceptional, loving, beings who lead more with their heart. Deep pre-angels have the ability to let go of the ego from a surface level. They can acknowledge the ego and drop it. They are able to lead with the heart (deep side) and choose more to lead with the heart than the ego. They only want what's best for themselves and others and are loving, helpful, and giving. They have a teacher and student attitude that shows in their actions of everyday living. They have a higher invisible vibrational energy, which many are attracted to like a magnet; pre-angels start asking them for advice about situations. Deep pre-angels concentrate on peace, spirituality, healthy living, loving themselves, new age therapy, acceptance, supporting others, and living in the now. Deep pre-angels give unconditional love to everyone, including themselves. When we become deep pre-angels, we are discovering who we are. We become trustworthy pre-angels who have a great appreciation for life and can identify our needs.

Spirituality

What is spirituality? Spirituality is a lifestyle choice of always leading with the heart and incorporating deep sided therapies and exercises in everyday lives. It is essential to understand that we need to achieve balance using the deep side of existence that will lead us to peace.

Being a spiritual pre-angel is becoming deep in our existence. It is not the same as being involved with a particular religion. Spirituality is an inner feeling of peace in the heart that has a living relationship with a higher power by believing in the universe, God, nature, or a higher power, whatever word that you give to the divine. Spirituality is a known unconscious place of peace and balance which guides us in our life journey in this dimension. Many pre-angels are coming to a realization in their lives that they want more and need to better understand life. Spirituality is the freedom of believing what we want to believe and creating our own philosophy of life.

We invest so much money into building our logical side so it becomes strong, but in the process we forget the deep side of existence. We need to invest in both sides. The logical side can be built up with education, work, science and ego. To strengthen the deep side, we have to educate ourselves and incorporate what we learn into our lives. Research, retreats, and other deep side therapies can be used to enhance this. The deep side involves getting to know who you are and loving yourself unconditionally.

Understanding the Life Dimension

We are each born with a soul, heart, spirit, body and mind; this is a breakdown of how we are built. While many pre-angels think the soul and spirit are the same thing, they actually are separate entities with different meanings. The soul is your purpose, which must be completed in order to return to heaven. The spirit is what makes you, you. It's your personality, actions, expressions, character, the way you act and talk, and, most of all, your identity. The heart is a piece of heaven. We only do peaceful, incredible actions using our hearts. The body is the physical part of you that shelters and holds your spirit, heart and soul in a human form. The mind is filled with information from both the logical and deep side. The left side of the mind is the logical side; it focuses on the surface, ego, work, education, and money. The right side relates to the heart, emotions, creativity and peace. It is essential to have balance and to lead slightly with the heart; when we do this, we are returning to the beginning of when we were born.

Picture This

Let's just say there was a friend of mine, who was employed at a factory where she assisted employees and former employees with occupational disease claims. At one point in her career, the amount of money that families were getting was in the hundreds of thousands of dollars. The company was losing money, so the boss asked her to adjust various occupational disease reports, requesting her to trim some of the dates where each employee worked. These dates were critical as they determined if the claim would go through or be denied and how much compensation would be given to the employees' family. The boss offered a bonus if she would complete the requests and sign her name to all documents. The young lady was hesitant, knowing that this was wrong. Although she would be helping out the company, she just didn't feel right doing this. All those innocent pre-angels and their families were suffering. She decided to lead with her heart and declined the offer. Unfortunately, she lost her job shortly after for unknown reasons. The woman led with her heart but she felt the injustice. It was wrong to let her go, so she contacted the manager above her boss and explained that she would expose them if they did not follow what she wanted. She led with the heart and also followed through with the logical side of surviving in this world. The company was afraid of what the young lady would do so she had to sign a confidentiality agreement. They offered her a severance package that only managers received. The union was shocked that the company was offering her so many things. They even changed her record of employment to show laid off. Her record of employment online showed changes from the company seven times, an indication that they were covering something up. Shortly after she found out that the company hired another pre-angel to do her same job. She

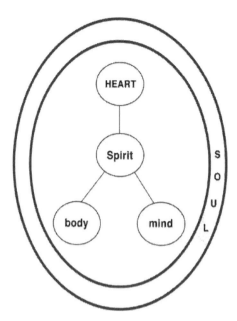

Figure 1: The Soul Connection

sees the same pre-angels who were involved with her firing and they just put their heads down when they pass by her in the city. Many of them have lost their hair and have aged through the five years that have passed.

We all have to survive in this world. The survival mode is from our logical side, but we need more peace, and money can't buy that. To find peace we must have balance with the logical side *and* the deep side.

The Soul Connection

A more detailed explanation of deep pre-angels is shown in Figure 1: The Soul Connection. Everyone born starts off loving, free and balanced. At this stage in our lives, we are complete, fearless, happy and balanced. This figure visually shows how we are at the beginning. Solid lines represent a connection to the other sources. The soul is peaceful, as indicated by solid lines. The solid lines are firm, accepting and connected. To understand why pre-angels do what they do, we will need to understand this figure first.

Soul

The soul has a solid line that indicates a connection to our purpose and demonstrates that our purpose is reachable. We have everything we need to achieve our purpose in this life. We need the body, spirit, heart, and mind to have solid lines to achieve our purpose.

Heart

The "Heart" encompasses the deepness that pre-angels need to feel fulfilled in the deep side. In this figure, the heart is at the top, meaning it leads everything. The heart connects to the right brain which leads with love, happiness and, compassion, and is always peaceful. The heart has a joining solid line underneath to demonstrate that the heart and spirit always go hand and hand; they are the driving force to the deep side of spirituality.

The Spirit

The spirit allows us to give the heart what it needs to lead. The spirit and heart have solid lines, so whatever the heart does, the spirit will follow. The spirit will communicate using an absolute loving style and peaceful way that we display using the senses. Our spirit is our identity.

The Mind

The "mind" in the figure indicates only the left (logical) side of the body. The mind in this figure has solid lines. Therefore, the ego is acknowledged but let go; it is not leading but follows. We always need to connect with the mind to survive in this dimension. The mind follows what the heart needs, therefore needs lead more than wants. The wants (logical side) and the needs (deep side) are balanced. In this figure, though, the heart has complete control over the mind. Therefore, only positive, peaceful words are displayed.

The Body

The body is connected with solid lines to imply that the body follows what the heart commands. It shows loving, touching actions. Our body here is pure and happy, no judgment or changes are recognized, and the body is a physical source.

When everything is balanced it will result in peace. This is a good indication that we are at a stage in our life that is back to the beginning. When we have balance, the universe will allow everything to fall into place, resulting in what "is meant to be".

As said early in the chapter, to increase deepness of the deep side, we can explore and do various deep side therapies and exercises. These deep therapies will help us to create balance, seek out who we are and fulfill the "needs" in our lives.

Deep Side Therapies & Exercises

Pre-angels who work with deep side therapies should have credentials in Metaphysic, Peace, and Spirituality. Some accredited schools offer specialty courses in these areas. To teach deep side therapies, individuals should have experience in applying deep side therapies to their own lives. At times certain spiritual pre-angels have supernatural gifts (read auras, intuitional healer, medium, psychic abilities). Through the use of these gifts they can give guidance as to what therapies or exercises can be done to resolve issues. These are called "moment treatments" and serve as a channeling of deep side therapies, including but not limited to:

Affirmations	Herbs & Healthy eating	Paying it forward
Alternative Therapy	Intimacy	Peace & Spiritual Mentor
Aromatherapy	Journaling	Reflexology
Be the Teacher	Law of Attraction	Reiki or Massage
Be near Water / Ocean	Life Coach	Retreats
Craniofacial Therapy	Me Time	Self-help books
Crystal Healing	Meditation	Spiritual Counseling
Detachment Therapy	Music Therapy	Vision Boards
Drawing & Coloring	Naturopathy	Volunteering
Dream work	Nature	Walking
Gemstone Therapy	Past Life Regression	Yoga or Tai Chi

Teaching One

It is important to note that our hearts are slightly to the left of our chests; therefore we should lead slightly with our heart (55%) when making decisions and living life. We should incorporate deep sided therapies & exercises into our lifestyle to achieve this balance which in the end will grant us peace.

CHAPTER 2

Logical Pre-angels

"When the mind leads ... War starts
When the heart leads ... Peace begins"
~ Fidgal

EINSTEIN STRESSED THAT THE logical side has to be acknowledged as it plays a key role in our existence and survival, here in the learning world that we call earth. He believed his purpose was to expose the energy of science from a logical side. Each time Jesus explained something to me and I didn't understand he would explain again using another learning style. Einstein was different; he believed that if you didn't get it after three times, then go do something to take your energy away from the problem and return when your energy has shifted. If the problem is a logical problem, do a deep side therapy or exercise then return to the problem with a much clearer understanding. So we would dance, walk in the forest and sometimes pick berries.

The ego has many terms in this book: the logical side, surface pre-angels or leading with the left side.

They all mean the same thing. Logical side also represents mother earth and the human side of our existence. There are different meanings of the word ego, and many use it as an acronym. Ego in this book means "Edging Gratitude Out". The ego refers to your conscious mind, rational side and the part of your identity that you consider your "self". In this book when I refer to logical pre-angels it means that they lead more with the logical side and at times the ego takes over.

"We allow the voice of the enemy to speak louder than the true voice"

~ Fidgal

In this book, a logical pre-angel is defined as one leading his or her life with more of the logical side, focusing on education, science, material possessions and money. The logical side is important, as it is the protection we need to survive in this world. We need to wake up in the morning and work so we can make money and eat. When we lead with the logical side, we are living in the past and/or are planning the future. When focusing on the logical side (pre-angels) only have a surface level vibration, a superficial approach to living and are using the ego to lead.

Logical pre-angels are not ready to live in the moment, so they put up barriers. The ego is a disconnection of their authentic self. All pre-angels are logical at some point in their lives.

The majority of our work and education is based on these logical approaches; they are institutionalized when we are children. Society has focused on the logical approach as a means of happiness and success with regards to money and power. We have given the logical side power and energy that we pretend enhances our lives. This behavior has been conditioned in us through work and school.

Many pre-angels, especially worthy ones, have a lack of fulfillment, a hole in their heart, so to speak. This is because their lives are successful from the logical perspective, but they are lacking something on the deep side.

Let's face it, we live in a more logical world where technology has taken over and made it more difficult to live in the now. It was different when the great philosophers were alive. Philosophers were brave pre-angels (deep) who lived in the moment. Now, we often multitask and constantly look at our cell phones. In the 1980s, pre-angels lived more in the now because they were forced to; there were no cell phones and there was significantly less technology. Technology can be a great tool to live in the now, with seeing our loved ones from afar. However, when we are with others, we should understand that when we glance at our cell phones we are not really with them. We are with our cell phones. We are not living in the now. If we want to create lasting memories, then we should have a time-boundary approach to using our cell phones and other technology. We should take a specific time to use our cell phones or leave them at home.

Picture This

Pre-angels are standing and watching a concert while they are texting. They text their friends that they love the concert. "Wish you were here. :)". Then they start looking at other text messages from friends and start texting them too. Is this living in the moment? The moment has past because the concert was passing while they were texting. Many of us are not living in the moment; we are living in the past because it flies by and we do not even remember it or acknowledge the feeling. If we were living in the now, then after the concert is over, we could write a good description of what we felt and how the concert was enjoyed.

We are living in a world that focuses on money, ego and the "what I want" approach, which is evidenced by what we have in our lives. Many logical pre-angels seem to have everything (material possessions, power, and money) but they feel something is missing in their lives. Not knowing what is missing or how to find it, they continue to search and live on the logical side, and continue to buy more stuff.

We are using the logical side to resolve world issues, and we are receiving logical results that are not sustaining us. These are called quick fixes and they are a duct tape approach to resolutions. When we decide to lead with the logical side when making decisions we feel happy and secure at first, but later the sustainability of that decision wears off, leaving us with a feeling of emptiness, resulting in dissatisfaction. Then we again focus on the wants approach and continue with this want cycle, which still does not give us satisfaction and happiness. Most logical pre-angels complain about their life and over analyze it. In their minds, they want to change, but need a push to do so. Changes are not wanted; they are needed. We will continually repeat the same type of logical behavior by using the want approach, choosing logical stuff and still feeling unfulfilled, until we realize that our needs must be addressed. Our needs are the deep sidedness that we must have in order to feel fulfilled. When we start taking different roads, we will get different results and a more deep side understanding of the life we need.

When logical pre-angels have a crisis or tragedy in their family, another logical pre-angel will not be able to provide the emotional response and support for them. They will feel the need to connect with a deep pre-angel. This can bring them to a higher invisible vibrational energy and they relate to them. A deep pre-angel will understand and not be judgmental.

When parents have children that are ill, the parents can become deep pre-angels because of their situation. They are forced to face the truth, which is to lead with their heart and find hope. Also, when a loved one has passed away, a logical pre-angel can shift and become a deep pre-angel. The emotions and the need to understand life comes from the loss. They start becoming a deep pre-angel and let go of ego and surface friends around them. At this point, they are more attracted to deep pre-angels. The universe then knows that the former logical pre-angel is ready to change and starts putting deep pre-angels in their lives.

Temporary Deepness

Logical pre-angels do not always focus on the logical side (ego). At times they lead with the heart, especially on occasions such as the birth of a child, a wedding or other special events, a family crisis, an illness, or a crisis of spirit. At other times, especially at Christmas, the spirit of the season is released and it becomes a time for logical pre-angels to lead with their hearts and give more. Many logical pre-angels become deep at Christmas. When a logical pre-angel becomes deep sided for a certain amount of time because of a crisis, during certain seasons and happy times, this is called **Temporary Deepness.** At this point, a shift of consciousness from a low vibration to a higher deeper vibration will occur. At times these individuals can be very warm pre-angels, and then the next day return to being their old selves – logical sided.

Logical pre-angels are more concerned with material possessions and money, and it takes away from them living in the now and fulfilling their lives. When logical pre-angels cannot find or do not see their purposes, oftentimes they will have a crisis of spirit, resulting in the need to find peace and balance. The more we have, the more we have to put our energy towards. Simple equals peace and peace equals a deeper connection to self. When we want to change and find peace the ego will disappear more rapidly.

The ego starts "sneaky mole" patterns full of little nagging thoughts, wandering, thinking of past mistakes, and voices in our heads that dominate us. We start believing them more and more. Self-doubt hits and picks at us. At times, when the ego takes over our lives 100%, we start believing in dark forces like the devil. The devil is a creation in our minds which can destroy our lives. We are taken over by unknown behaviors and we start becoming someone who we do not even recognize or like. The universe will always provide pre-angels and other messages to help us get through this state of mind of the devil. This 100% ego takeover can be difficult to overcome, but we need to get back on track by leading with the heart.

Over time, the logical answers will not fulfill what's in our heart. These consistent results create unhappiness, stress, dissatisfaction, and depression (attachment). Pre-angels all need more in life and to achieve this we must make changes to better the process. Everyone will get more in life if they lead more with their hearts. When the heart leads, peace starts, and everything will fall into place, and fulfillment will vibrate. The logical side must be acknowledged and let go of. Yes, in certain situations that are life threatening you need the logical side to prevail and to lead. When an injury occurs, the logical side should lead and get medical attention. However, it is important to note that anyone can change at any time in their minds and decide to be a deeper pre-angel. For logical pre-angels it may take some time for that change because they have to let go of the ego and remove the notion of material possessions and money.

Picture This

If you are being attacked, you need to lead more with the logical side to defend yourself from the attack. Then once you are safe and healed, you can send love to the attacker.

～

There is a saying that says when one hangs around with wolves, one will become a wolf. If you hang around with logical pre-angels then you will start being like them. Logical pre-angels like to hang out with logical pre-angels. It's because their invisible vibrational energy matches, so the energy creates a feeling of belonging and understanding. Logical pre-angels enjoy being in a clique, and will always invite other logical pre-angels to join. However, as soon as any member no longer meets the logical level of invisible energy vibration criteria, then that member is removed from the clique. Deep pre-angels are not usually involved with these cliques.

Sometimes logical pre-angels lead with the logical side because they are confused with messages that the universe is giving them and cannot distinguish between these messages and the ego. How do we distinguish between the two? Anything that gives only yourself a gain is the ego talking. There are certain feelings that disguise as the ego. If it's not peaceful to your soul and others then it's the ego. Choosing discipline today can create a removal of the ego; we must refrain from temptation. Having discipline will create sustainability in our lives. Ego will tell us to be rude. Ego always wants to be comfortable and will never grow spiritually. Fewer consequences will create less conflict in our lives when we remove the ego.

"Those who pay the price for discipline
will be rewarded in the future"
~ Fidgal

To sustain our lives, we need both the logical and deep sides for a natural source of everything to flow; balance is the key. Our minds should always work in loving service to our soul, and that's how we lead with our hearts.

Logical Side Therapies & Exercises

Professionals providing logical side therapies usually have credentials from universities. Some professionals may incorporate deep side practices into their therapies; this is good but is limited to some deep sided therapies. Sometimes deep therapies require supernatural abilities (read auras, intuitional healer, medium, psychic abilities), in order to give the right guidance of therapy or treatment. We should remember that logical pre-angels will attend logical institutions; therefore, deep side therapies will not be part of their credentials. Here are some logical sided therapies and activities that can help with achieving the 45%.

Chiropractor	Join a sports team	Ride a bike
Cognitive Behavioral Therapy	Marijuana (moderation)	Read Magazines
Craniosacral therapy	Mathematics	Rehabilitation
Clean the house	Occupational therapist	Sex
Donate money to charity	Osteopathy	Shopping
Drink socially	Prescription medication	Support groups
Exercise	Psychologist	Traditional counseling
Family doctor	Psychotherapy	Watch a sports game
Gamble (moderation)	Puzzles	Watch television

Understanding Soul Disconnection

We are exposed to different levels of logical pre-angels. Some logical pre-angels are logical closed minded and only lead with a one-sided approach to life. They are not open to anything else in the universe, and are usually defined as having a ridged, rule-based personality with a no fun attitude and low invisible vibrational energy. Their direct approach needs everything to be proven by science or data in order for them to believe. Then there are logical pre-angels who are logical open minded.

These pre-angels believe in data but are curious, open minded to new opportunities, and focused on education but disbelieve if not given facts to support it. When we are talking logical pre-angels, we are talking of those who live their lives at ego level vibration, leading more with the logical mindset. They have a disconnection with the soul and heart. The logical side of the mind (ego, surface) represents money, power, credentials, scientific approach, education and surface level behavior.

The logical side of pre-angels may have other surface behaviors including gossip, negative words, hurtful actions, selfishness, the blame game, an all about me attitude and addictions (drug, alcoholics, workaholics). Another type of unsettling behavior is continuously bringing up the past and joking about it over and over again. They will put themselves on pedestals. This kind of approach has to do with stroking the ego. Many logical pre-angels are unhappy in their lives and will find alternative ways to promote happiness but this is not really happiness. This is just stroking the ego and is called **artificial happiness.** Artificial happiness never lasts and will be seen by many as being fake.

The Soul Disconnection

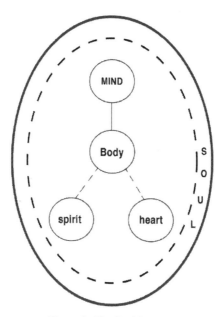

Figure 2: The Soul Disconnection

A more detailed explanation is shown in Figure 2: The Soul Disconnection figure. It illustrates and explains what a logical pre-angel is like from a visual perspective. To understand why pre-angels do what they do, we need to gain a thorough understanding of how our life dimension works using the logical side and deep side thinking. In this figure, when a soul is disconnected from self, the soul's purpose is no longer acknowledged.

This figure shows the pre-angel developing a disconnection from their soul, spirit and heart. This can happen for many reasons, leading with not believing in themselves, focusing on money and buying material possessions, and allowing ego to take over. And lastly, fear always comes into play in this learning world that we call earth. Fear is an illusion that we accept from the ego point of view. Because logical pre-angels have a disconnection with the heart, they may say or do hurtful things. They can say harsh words and be resentful when actions are directed to them.

Committing Suicide

At times, the soul would like to move into another body and restart. This is evident in suicidal thoughts. When the ego leads, sometimes life gets put on hold; the pre-angel feels overwhelmed and loses track of his/her purpose. In contrast to the Soul Connection figure 1, the dotted lines indicate a disconnect and jumps at times to being connected when we make certain changes in our lives. When the soul is attached for a moment, it can change the whole figure, and a pre-angel can be back on track and return to a similar state of when they were born (as shown in the Soul Connection figure 1.0). If the ego takes over, the heart and spirit are disconnected from existence. Many family and friends say that the pre-angel is different and that they cannot understand or like them at this stage. When the mind leads 100%, a disconnection with the heart and soul occurs, and the mind subconsciously hears messages that the individual might misinterpret. This misinterpretation can appear as suicidal thoughts, anger issues, and violent actions.

When the logical side leads 90-100%, out of character responses will occur and subconsciously, messages will be mixed. Instead of hearing "Johnny, look at that beautiful view on the bridge," Johnny hears "Johnny go and jump off the bridge." When this occurs, a domino effect happens with the heart and spirit continuously disconnecting. The body, on the other hand, is attached and follows direct orders from the mind, which is why the solid lines between the body and mind are displayed in Figure 2: The Soul Disconnection. The same figure can help us to understand why pre-angels commit suicide. When the more severe aspects of the mind lead, the results can be disastrous. Fidgal explained to me one has to be so strong to be able to kill themselves. Have you ever heard the saying, "I was there but I wasn't there"? This is what happens when someone commits suicide.

Violence

When we hear of terrible violent crimes, it is difficult to understand how a pre-angel could commit such acts. Many pre-angels say that it is out of character for this pre-angel to commit such violence. This is what happens, though, when the logical side leads 100%. When the logical side takes over, the individual is unaware of what's going on in his/her mind. A rampage is in full force, and they do not have the ability to stop. When the logical side leads, the pre-angel is on a roller coaster ride and does not have the capacity to stop. At times when the logical side leads (100%), a negative demeanor develops, including anger, bad behavior, crimes, and actions that are not usually part of the individual's character. This is where the phrase brainwash comes into play. They feel detached from their heart and feel emotionally unavailable. The logical side is uncontrollable at this stage, and the body just follows the request of the logical mind. The mind presents itself as a powerful force that tricks the pre-angel into thinking that he or she can get away with anything. This is the ego talking and feeling powerful. As a result of the logical mind leading, pre-angels could start shooting others in public. At times, the pre-angel who committed the crime doesn't understand or even remember what they have done.

Picture This

When the logical mind is leading 100% and a pre-angel plays violent video games, the logical mind (ego) can get confused and start thinking what they just played is reality. They become brainwashed and feel the need to protect themselves from the outside so when fear appears they start shooting. In this case, the ego has taken over, and there is a disconnection between the heart and soul.

Teaching Two

The logical side does have to be recognized temporarily and let go. We should allow the logical side to follow using 45%. If one attaches too much to the logical side, then illusion will take over. We need both the logical and deep sides to balance and find peace, for using only one will not maintain life.

CHAPTER 3

Crisis of Spirit

"Not everyone who is lost is depressed".
~ Fidgal

As said at the beginning, Einstein and Jesus expressed concern for the future and gave these teachings to assist recovery from crises. They both insisted that if both logical and deep side therapies and exercises are not part of our daily lives, a crisis will occur. The more imbalanced the world is and the more years go by, pre-angels will become lost more often in their lives and at an earlier age. When lost, we are having a crisis of spirit but we have a great likelihood for recovery. In this chapter, we will learn what happens when balance is not achieved.

Crisis of Spirit

A **Crisis of Spirit** is an imbalance leading to 80% from one side, the deep or logical side which causes an identity crisis. This may lead one to think about a mid-life crisis which often occurs in pre-angels 45 to 55 years old. A mid-life crisis is a crisis of spirit that commonly occurs at that age as the ultimate built up from mini crises that we have not dealt with at that time of our lives. A crisis of spirit is not limited to mid-life. It can occur at any time in our life.

To resolve this type of crisis we must incorporate the therapies and exercises from the opposite side of that which is leading with the 80%. A crisis of spirit encompasses the numerous mini crises that we have never dealt with in our lives and in our past lives. At this stage pre-angels can feel empty, without a purpose, have no sense of identity, and experience a self-confidence downturn. Everything is put on hold; they become not like themselves. At times, they do not go to work, are sad and stop the deep and logical side approaches to living their lives.

In a logical crisis of spirit, the logical side leads 80%, and the deep side follows at 20%. In this logical crisis of spirit, many strange behaviors will appear. With this crisis, the deep side is not being recognized enough and the need to feel love and follow the heart must be addressed. Deep side therapies and exercises will be required.

When pre-angels get depressed, they are attaching themselves to emotions and leading 80% with the deep side (heart), and 20% with the logical side. When this occurs, it is called a deep crisis of spirit. This deepness can lead to little ego being recognized and attachment or depression sets in. The logical side is not able to address the survival mode of living on earth. They can't get out of bed, can't go to work, so they can't make money and do daily life activities. They end up sleeping a lot and feeling sad. With this crisis, the logical side is not being recognized enough and logical therapies and exercises are required.

Quarterly Crisis

Many young adults have quarterly crisis around the age of 25. They finish school, and start in the workforce, and all of sudden do not like their career or life. They feel like something is missing. Finishing school and having too much debt can cause this quarterly crisis. In other instances, they may not finish school because they don't know who they are or what to take in school. They are in a phase where they are lost and decide to do nothing. The quarterly crisis causes a ripple effect in the medical industry, as medication is prescribed to help these young pre-angels with depression. The quarterly crisis is being misdiagnosed as depression, when what pre-angels in this state actually need is to focus on who they want to be now. Unfortunately, society is focusing too much on the path of getting credentials and going to work, and when individuals do not do this in a certain order doctors, parents and other professionals think they are depressed.

Throughout our lives education is based on the logical side of thinking. There are more logical programs in the school system than deep programs. Having too much logic and leading with it causes a "want" approach and does not fulfill our needs. It is important to note that we need to start educating young pre-angels to understand that spirituality and being deep is the solution to fulfilling the gap in their lives. We have hearts, but we are not using them to our full potential of love. If we used our hearts to make this world a better place, then no one would starve. Everyone wants peace, but to get it they are focusing on the logical side. Unfortunately, there is no logical side of being peaceful; deep is represented from a heart point of view.

We have been conditioned to see logical pre-angels like doctors for answers, so we accept medication that gives us logical results. There is more to life than the logical side. It is when we are depressed and lost that exploring alternative therapy in the deep side and the spiritual world will benefit us.

From a logical side, many experience a crisis of spirit and are diagnosed and given medication which they believe is needed. However, medication alone will not fully treat this crisis. It will only address half of the problem. To resolve this crisis of spirit, we need treatments from both the medical field and from spiritual mentors. That's why medication is not working for many, and doctors have to change their medication. One side is being sustained, that's only 45%, while the other side (the deep side) is at zero. Both logical and deep treatments will maintain us through any crisis of spirit. We need both to achieve balance, and then we will become peaceful.

Picture This

Priests think they are deep pre-angels using religion as the means to be deep and with no ego recognized. Priests have learned to be 80%-100% deep using religion as the means to understand life, leaving 0-20% for the logical side. This is an imbalance. When you have an imbalance, consequences occur. There has been much in the news about some Roman Catholic priests caught abusing children. Priests are forbidden to have sex, get married, which is causing a side effect to the logical side. This side effect could cause them to abuse children. Priests should have a wife and children; this would give them the experience as a teacher to understand what other couples go through. We can learn so much from reading books, but we need to experience it too. We have to be the teacher and the student, and we need to learn in a logical way and in a practical way too. Priests go to school to learn only from a lecture perspective but most have not experienced what they are teaching. This kind of behavior will continue if there is no balance in the logical and deep sides. To find peace and balance, we need the logical (ego) at 45% to fulfill the wants from a logical point of view.

Song Reference:
The Face by RyanDan

Indecisive Stage

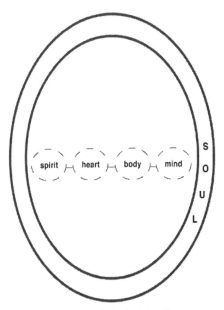

Figure 3: Indecisive Stage

When we have a crisis of spirit, we tend to get lost and stuck in a comfortable non-action zone. This is the one that most pre-angels seem to stay in during their lifetime, either because they are not motivated, are lost, or they just don't know where to go for help.

Figure 3: Indecisive stage shows that no life entity is leading, and the pre-angel is lost or is a state of convenience. At this stage in the pre-angel's life they have lost their identity, both the logical and the deep side of living and have put everything on hold. They are undecided on how to live their life, either leading with the logical mind or the deep (heart), so they do nothing at times. When one is going through this stage, depression has an increasing chance of presenting itself. In this phase, pre-angels go from one extreme to another, commonly known as mood swings. They can lead 80% with the logical side and then dramatically switch and lead with the deep side (80%). This can occur repeatedly, and it is unknown when it will stop. It also shows when a pre-angel is indecisive in the midst of everything that is happening around them and they choose to stay in a holding stage by choosing to do nothing. Many would call this stage as being "stuck". During a period of being stuck, an individual will feel empty and their mind, body, spirit and heart will be disconnected. They will not understand who they are. Triggers may include a dead relationship, a tragedy occurring, and disconnection with a career. This stuck phase develops over time, a time of comfort and convenience, a time of not dealing with situations, emotions, and not dealing with the challenges of everyday life.

Picture This

Often, when someone is unhappy in their marriage, he/she will continue to stay in the marriage and live a lie over and over even though they know that they are not happy or growing. They choose to do nothing, as their relationship is routine and comfortable. Avoidance is a form of coping that many logical pre-angels use and believe. However, avoidance is not a coping skill; it is an artificial way of dealing with conflicts and may lead to addictions. Pre-angels in this phase can develop different personalities, going back and forth between varying behavior patterns. Individuals need to make positive changes, and become motivated to lead using the heart, with the ego in check.

In the decisive stage, the key is finding out who you want to be now.

Song Reference:
***This is Your Life* by Switchfoot**

Depression

The other side of the crisis of spirit is having too much deepness in life, causing depression. From a deep side definition, depression is an attachment. It can be a result of not dealing with emotions. It is the side effect of not dealing with anger that has built up over time. Then, the build-up becomes an attachment to emotions. We go from one extreme to another. At times pre-angels are misdiagnosed and think they are depressed, but instead they have an attachment issue. Attachment is when empathy takes over our lives. We attach ourselves to emotions, pre-angels, unhappiness, sad situations, worry, grief and being unable to forgive.

Procrastination

Because depression (attachment) can be so depleting and tiring, we tend to lose interest and not do the daily activities that help us survive. Many of our daily required activities, like getting out of bed, washing dishes, making dinner, and personal hygiene are difficult to accomplish. These activities are menial, but they help us survive and keep us healthy using the logical side of living. Some of the household and family duties will pile up and we get more stressed and depressed because we cannot complete them. We start procrastinating with everything and rushing frantically at times to get things done. The way to defeat this procrastination cycle and not feel so helpless is to take baby steps.

How can deep pre-angels return to balance? It's simple; recognize the logical side (ego). The ego will get the pre-angel out into society, attending events, out of bed and doing menial tasks. Then a detachment of the heart needs to be done. One has to hang out with logical pre-angels to bring their invisible vibration energy to boost their own logical level.

Exercise

Here is an exercise that will help you take charge of procrastination at a slow pace. Write down all the items that you feel you need to accomplish. Get some sticky notes and write each item on its own sticky note on the sticky side of the paper. On other sticky notes (again on the sticky side) write down some rewards you like, for example, go out for dinner, and go to the spa. Mix the rewards sticky notes with the sticky notes of items that you have to complete. Stick them to a wall so you do not see the writing. No peeking! Each week or day pick one of the sticky notes to complete. Sometimes planning has to be involved and research has to be done in order to finish the task. Be gentle with yourself and just do it. It doesn't matter how fast you get there, it's that you get there. This exercise will help to get many things completed and will contribute to building up the logical side.

Teaching Three

It is important to understand when someone is leading too much either with the logical or deep side

then a crisis of spirit, also known as an identity crisis will occur. Furthermore, we must seek professional help using both types of treatment (logical, deep) to achieve balance again. To resolve this type of crisis we must incorporate the therapies and exercises from the opposite side of that which is leading with the 80%. We must reset ourselves to become aware of living in the now.

Careers

Contributing to the crisis of spirit could be your career. In this learning world we call earth, we need to survive. For the majority of pre-angels, that means that we have to work and spend more than 50% of our day working and the rest living. In today's world, many pre-angels take jobs just to pay the bills. Sometimes if someone is focused on their passion and cannot do it, they too will have a crisis of spirit. What pre-angels should be doing is working in a career that rewards their purpose and brings them happiness. Unfortunately, many times this does not happen because we need money to survive.

In the previous chapter, it was explained that pre-angels will resurface on earth if they did not complete their purpose. So if we apply this notion, that means seven billion pre-angels have not fulfilled their purpose in this world. Once we find our purpose, everything in the universe will fall into place (happiness, money, and real love). This is called the "**bliss**" stage and can be achieved if we have balance. If pre-angels are taking jobs just to survive, then many are unhappy. Unhappiness causes attachment issues that could lead to depression and other behavioral problems.

Giving Back

Pre-angels who have found their purpose and are passionate about what they're doing tend to give it away for free at times. Providing services for free is a good way of leading with the heart. However, from a logical side, when services are free they are not valued as much. We should accept other pre-angel's generosity, and start receiving their services in a peaceful way without questioning the authenticity. We can then give it back through providing aid to others who are in need. When we give, the universe will give us back in return.

Negative Impact Jobs

A **negative impact job** is a job in which we must provide a service that the receivers feel is negative. The public who receives that service then responds negatively to the individual, creating a vicious cycle of negative energy. Sometimes negative impact jobs have to be taken in order to survive in this world.

Picture This

A middle-aged man who needs to make some money becomes a parking attendant. Despite not caring about parking laws, he takes a job as a parking attendant just to pay the bills. He is required to give a certain amount of tickets per day, which, of course is disliked by the pre-angels he gives tickets to. He doesn't enjoy his job at all. This is a negative impact career. At times in our lives we all have negative impact careers. In any job, we can look at the bright side and try to do the duties in a peaceful way. Giving tickets is a nasty job but someone has to do it. If the parking attendant meets his quota then give second chances to someone whose time has expired, he would lead with his heart and better the job.

Shadow Behaviors

If we have logical jobs with primarily logical duties, we must work towards having a deep side in our home lives to maintain a balance. This also applies to deep jobs; we must incorporate logical activities on the home front to maintain balance. If we work in negative impact jobs, we have to find ways to be happy outside of work. This involves detachment. With negative impact jobs, we must prevent ourselves from bringing home the mess that we endured at work. If we do not detach from negative impact jobs, then we may shadow the behavior we have witnessed and take on the issues and energy of others. Mirroring the behaviors and actions of what we have seen in a negative impact job is called **shadow behavior.**

Picture This

If a police officer hears a lot of foul comments at his work place, then he/she may continue to replay them in his/her head at home. It's easy to let work continue to dominate our home lives and thus create an imbalance. It is possible for those who have a negative impact career to not allow their job to take over the rest of their lives. Pre-angels in this situation need to detach and let it go. If they do not detach then they will take the energy from work into their home then shadow behavior may occur. In this practical example, a police officer may say foul comments in the home. The home will become tainted with that same energy from work and a domino effect will occur with everyone in the home.

Toxic Work Environment

A toxic work environment develops from the employees who make up this atmosphere. It's all about who is hiring the employees. If a hiring committee is more logical, then they will seek a logical candidate. Many employers are using a point system in place during interviews. This system is a poor system that is designed to seek qualified candidates from the logical side to do the job. But it doesn't determine what type of pre-angel they are with respect to personality and beliefs that fit in with the organization. Unfortunately, there are policies and procedures on what to ask during an interview and they have to be honored based on the laws.

In a work place that has too many pre-angels leading with logic, there will be many unbalanced pre-angels. An invisible vibrational energy is created that many will attach themselves to and they too will become imbalanced. This will cause a crisis of spirit in the work place environment leaving many pre-angels to take stress leaves, costly medical leaves that are difficult to resolve, as they are personal crises.

Suggested Solution

In order to resolve and achieve a peaceful work place environment, the hiring committee can create or purchase an emotional intelligence test that will capture their organization's behavior and meet their core values. Emotional intelligence testing can demonstrate a candidate's emotional state of mind, what drives their behavior and impacts them (positively and negatively). It can show how the candidate manages emotional stress while under pressure. The emotional state of mind is important because of the energy that it projects into the organization.

This testing can also show self-awareness and self-managing factors. There are many of these tests that are written and approved by accredited agencies and can be laid out in the job posting. Using emotional intelligence testing along with the point system will get the best candidate who will match the energy and benefit the organization in the long term. By doing both, it will sustain the organization down the line, saving money and maintaining a happier workplace. A happier workplace will have a domino effect in the employees' personal lives and morale will increase in the workplace.

It doesn't stop there: an organization should provide a deeper side approach to working and living. Jobs are mostly logical because rules have made them logical. If an organization incorporated deeper side activities then a more balanced atmosphere would develop and the organization could succeed. For example, an office could offer yoga during the day, meditation at certain times and other peace tools. Doing this will help the employee in their personal lives as well, gaining awareness and confidence resulting in employees taking less time off of work for stress management. These are simple but profound ways of sustaining a peaceful place within an organization. No one wants to go to an environment that is toxic and stale.

Let's face it. Many organizations will not incorporate emotional intelligence testing or other deep side activities. If we work in a logical environment then we have to find peace in our personal life. Start doing deep activities at home; use the right side of your mind. Be creative. Send love. Take a spa day. Meditate. Spend time with deep pre-angels. Do yoga. Volunteer. Make love and love yourself. We need balance in all areas of our lives and must take the responsibility to add what we need.

When we have balance the events that come up at work will be more manageable and we will be able to detach from the drama.

Bullying

For years bullying has been a factor in the school system. Now, on certain days, children, teachers, and many throughout the community wear pink to support anti-bullying. If we want to stop bullying, we need to teach our children how to stop bullying at home and in the workplace. How can we teach our children not to be bullies when we at work exclude certain pre-angels or gossip about them? Bullying can be defined in various ways (exclusion, harsh words, punching, etc.).

There is always someone in the workplace that at times is known as difficult. Managers know this and do nothing about it. The teachers in our school system are like managers. When a child is being bullied at school and they tell the teacher, the teacher must address the matter with the parents of both the child and the bully and come up with a plan to stop the bullying. What is going to happen when the child grows up and has someone who is bullying them in the workplace? They will tell their boss, but most times their boss will do nothing. This is what is happening in a lot of workplace environments. Many bosses do not have the skills to address this. Many organizations do not even address social exclusion in the policy and procedures manuals.

Bullying has much to do with anger. It could be anger from the past that has redeveloped and is brought into one's current life. Bullying is also a sign of sadness, a sign of missing something in their personal life, or jealousy that is held onto. It is a consciously negative energy causing harsh words to be said and hurtful actions.

Understand that bullying is like war. No one wins when there is a war. We need to educate adults, especially managers, about bullying. Bullying develops a toxic energy in the workplace that causes injury and stress. It is a big contributing factor to a negative impact career.

Anti-bullying must start with adults, not children. Children repeat the same actions and messages that they see, hear and feel from their parents. You cannot fool a child. They have the most intuitive energy that is higher than the adult's intuitive energy. Adults need to accept pre-angels for who they are, getting to know them and not judge them, for those who judge pre-angels are judging themselves.

Suggested Solution

For those who are the bully, there is an imbalance on the deep side. The bully needs to connect with the heart. Sometimes allowing a bully to spend time with someone who is different from him/herself will increase leading with the heart. This will teach her/him compassion and understanding. Continue doing more deep side activities until the bullying stops.

Attachment & Detachment

Einstein spoke passionately about energies attaching to objects, and to pre-angels. We have energy and we can hold on or pick up other pre-angel's energy if we do not live in the now. Einstein believed that everything is temporary and that we have to continue using this philosophy in order to detach ourselves from things in life. Here we will learn how to detach ourselves using the detachment model.

The past is not in the past if we bring it up in the present. From a deep side definition, depression is an attachment. What is an attachment? **Attachment** occurs when we connect to pre-angels, material possessions, emotions, money, energies, past lives and situations that take over our lives and keep us from ourselves. When we attach ourselves to anything, we are not living in the moment. This is an ego-driven behavior, and we will receive logical results over and over until we are ready to detach ourselves. Attachment doesn't provide us with any value; it gives us conflicts. Any attachment is an illusion that we have created through logical thinking. When we attach ourselves to anything we are not our authentic self, and it becomes harder to detach from what is surrounding us.

Signs of attachment include constantly talking about the same thing, thinking about it, stalking, overanalyzing, micromanaging, extreme empathy, and losing control of one's own life. The behavioral effects of attachment vary but include voices in your head, nausea, headaches, anxiety, sleeplessness, mood swings, snapping at pre-angels, unhappiness, compulsive behaviors, and obsession with certain items and events.

Pre-angels make choices, and we need to accept them and move on. Many attachments are controlling our lives. From a logical side, this can be classified as a disease with unknown side effects. Let us focus on the different attachments that many pre-angels have and learn how to detach.

"One will never be disappointed if one detaches to everything in life"
~ Fidgal

Figure 4: The Attachment Cycle

To understand more in depth about attachment, Figure 4 describes what occurs when we attach ourselves to something. We attach ourselves to stuff, energies, memories, pre-angels, and money, and expect certain actions will occur from attaching to these. When we do not get the results we want we get disappointed and feel sad, which can lead to depression or resentment. As a result, we feel unbalanced in our life, until we attach ourselves to something else. And the attachment cycle continues and continues. When we are unbalanced, it means we are leading from one extreme, either the logical side or the deep side, and we are unaware of messages around us and uncontrollable behaviors.

Some of the attachments that we will endure during our time here are the following: Past Life Memories, Emotions & Energy, and Material Possessions.

Past Life Memories

One attachment issue that many are suffering from is past life memories. Many pre-angels believe in reincarnation or rebirth. In heaven, they speak of this often and have given me the message that if we do not complete our purpose, we will return to earth to live again to fulfill our soul mission. **Past Life Memories** occur when we attach ourselves to something in either our childhood or from a past life. In a past life we did not resolve our issues before we died and so we brought them into this current life.

With past life memories we bring the characteristics of the attachment in a past life to our current life. With any past issues or trauma, some behavior will surface, and many pre-angels do not know why. The attachment problem that they had in their past lives has resurfaced from a trigger in this current life. As a result, we develop mental illnesses, medical and behavior issues that cannot be explained or completely treated. The logical pre-angels (scientific) have a different take on why we have mental illnesses, medical and behavior problems. They use a scientific understanding, such as data, genetics, and lifestyle to attempt to understand the medical conditions. <u>It's simpler on the deep side; we bring the attachment issues that were not dealt with in our past lives into our current life.</u>

What is happening is pre-angels are using only one means of treatment for the illness, which is the logical side. Simply using a logical treatment, however, is not working for past life memories and trauma. To resolve these attachment challenges, we need to treat with both logical and deep side therapies. Medication alone, which is a logical treatment, is not working for many and doctors are constantly changing their patients' medications. By using medications, the logical side is being sustained using 45%, while the deep side is left using zero. We must take it upon ourselves as patients to seek deep side therapies along with the medical logical treatment. Using both logical and deep side treatments will sustain pre-angels through any past life memories. We need both to achieve balance and peace. Using hypnosis and different forms of past life regression therapy will be helpful in determining what occurred in past lives. The treatment must happen in the now, in the present, in order to let go of the past events. It is a different but effective way of treating.

Picture This

A baby girl was born with a serious heart condition: three holes in her heart. From the deep side, it means in her past lives she had more than one broken heart and attached herself to the pain that the broken hearts gave her. She died before she could mend all those broken hearts. So when she was reborn, she brought the broken heart attachment to her current life. She had to go through open heart surgery as a baby and receive the greatest gift of all, healing from the heavens when she had her near-death experience. Both treatments were used: the logical side (surgery) and the deep (the heavens) to heal her heart.

Energy Attachment

Energies are around us, although they are not visible to the naked eye. When we take energy from other pre-angels or an event, it takes precedence over living in the now. Everyone has energy around them. Some call it an aura, and some call it an intuitive feeling. I've referred to it earlier as invisible vibrational energy. When a pre-angel meets another pre-angel for the first time, the first impression is created. This first impression is partly the result of feeling the other pre-angel's energy and using the seven senses to understand who they are. (We will discuss the seven senses in chapter five). When we do this, we attach ourselves to their energy and at times, bring our energy to their energy level.

Pre-angels can also accidentally pick up or steal energy from one another, which is comparable to a vampire sucking blood. Many pre-angels do not even know that they are doing this. Stealing or taking on someone's energy can occur when talking to someone, through Reiki or other energy healings. When someone with a lower vibrational energy interacts with someone of a higher vibrational energy they may accidentally pull some of the higher energy away from the other pre-angel. The pre-angel with the higher invisible vibrational energy unknowingly shares and can be left depleted.

When someone steals our energy, we may get the following side effects: exhaustion, nausea, headaches, dizziness and not feeling like ourselves.

To prevent our energy being stolen, we must protect it from others who are not at our level of energy. Usually, pre-angels that are at a lower energy lead more with the logical side. Be conscious of various pre-angels around you, if you feel that their energy is off, protect yourself. It's always best to surround yourself with positive pre-angels who have energies that match yours or are a bit higher.

There are many ways to protect our energies. One is creating an invisible white bubble around us and quietly repeating, "My energy is my energy and no one can go into my energy bubble." Sometimes, stomping our feet before we meet someone will protect our energy. The stomping vibrates into the ground to the roots of trees. Roots and trees are a natural grounding source to the universe. The best practice of keeping your energy is acknowledging it; just thinking of your energy projects it. If we understand attachment, then we can learn how to detach ourselves from other pre-angels' energies.

Those who work helping pre-angels with mental illness or medical problems have a higher risk of taking on their energy. They must protect their energies and learn how to detach themselves from the patient.

Picture This

A suicide prevention counselor working in a call center becomes the patient. They bring home the energy of that last caller. They match the caller's problems with their life and start attaching themselves to those problems. The sound of the pre-angel's voice stays in their head, the image that they create in their minds, the bad taste in their mouths, the touch of their feelings of emptiness, the smell of the familiar astrosphere, and the environment of where they are, and the intuitive energy that they feel is recognized. After time, if attachment is not prevented, then the suicide prevention counselor becomes the patient, or worse, commits suicide.

Material Possessions

Material possessions include stuff and money. Over the years, we see our parents buy stuff that builds up, until they must either give it away or have a garage sale. When we are not able to let go of our material possessions, we become attached to them. Money is the instigator of buying these possessions. If we didn't attach ourselves to money, then we would not have so much stuff. Money lets us survive in this world, but doesn't give us the 100% means of living; it just helps us to survive. Many pre-angels use money to provide missing elements in their lives. This is why many pre-angels who have a mid-life crisis or a crisis of spirit purchase expensive items. They believe that an article will satisfy the need that is missing in their life. This item is only a temporary fix for the missing element. Once they realize that the item is not fulfilling them, then they will return to the crisis, but hopefully understand this time that they are missing the deep side in their lives.

Some of us will save and save until life passes us by, and we haven't really enjoyed the money that was saved. The next quote applies to anything in our life. Coupons will expire, some items will get old and decay and some will get destroyed, pre-angels will die before using up their savings. We need to start using and enjoying what we have saved.

"Keep saving for one day,
you will not be able to use what you saved."
~ Fidgal

A substantial number of pre-angels who are saving and saving stuff become hoarders. Our lives are not meant to be filled with things, and our world should not be driven by stuff and attachment to them. We need money and stuff to survive, but when it takes over our lives then our lives are not our lives anymore. Yes, we should enjoy our material possessions. If we continue to save and save and not use it, then what was the meaning of saving it? If we lead with the heart, then no one in this world would go without food, water, shelter, and stuff. We have to have a surface approach to money and material possessions and start enjoying what we have saved and earned. USE IT!

Detachment is a peaceful way of loving ourselves and the only solution to attachment. Detachment involves living in the present moment; this is the means of balance in our life. Figure 5 shows how to separate from anything. When we learn how to detach, we love and care for ourselves first. It doesn't mean that we do not care for others; we just place healthy boundaries so as not to get attached and go insane. When we are detached, we have a better ability to make healthy decisions, and love pre-angels in a compassionate way. We also have greater appreciation for our lives.

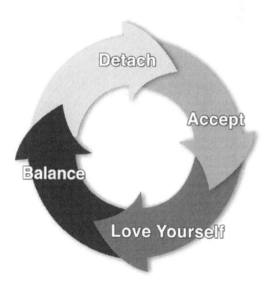

Figure 5: The Detachment Cycle

"When we let go, we allow life to happen."
~ Fidgal

One form of detachment is accepting reality. It requires accepting our past choices. When we truly accept these decisions we will not blame ourselves or others, but learn from these decisions, as well as understand destiny and feel free to live in the moment. Figure 5 outlines how to detach from anything. To detach, we must accept what has happened by taking responsibility for our choices and love ourselves again by finding out who we are now and who we want to be. Then we become balanced again.

Detachment Solutions

There are three detachment solutions that we can use in our everyday lives. These include loving ourselves, placing healthy and realistic boundaries, and having less information. To use these detachment solutions, we must apply them to each attachment issue.

Loving Ourselves

When we attach ourselves, we start acting like someone else and our energy and spirit are depleted. We owe it to ourselves to love ourselves unconditionally. We can care for someone without getting attached to the drama in their lives and our minds. We must love ourselves first, and then we can continue to give healthy love to others. There are many services that we can tap into to help with their care; we do not have to do it all ourselves.

From time to time, we want to save pre-angels from pain, and we give empathy to them. What we should be giving is sympathy. The two are very different, and many pre-angels have different interpretations of these two words. Fidgal explained that empathy is taking on the inner vibration (energy) of another. When we are empathetic, we attach ourselves to their drama, and subconsciously start believing that their problems are our problems now. But when we give empathy, we lead only with the heart, which can result in a depression. At times we get confused and think we can save them, but saving is not loving. What we need to give is sympathy. Sympathy (compassion) recognizes our feelings towards a situation or pre-angel by using a borderline approach, rather than taking on their energy. We can recognize this by acknowledging feelings and then letting them go.

"When we are not authentic, it is harder
to detach ourselves from what is surrounding us"
~ Fidgal

"Me time" is a good way of loving ourselves and getting to know who we are. It's necessary for aligning ourselves with living in the now and making ourselves happy. If we love ourselves, we will be able to let go of anything that makes us unhappy. We can learn to focus on happiness and pre-angels who are positive and match our invisible vibrational energy, while we send love to those that are not in a good place from a distance. If we accept everyone as they are, then we will not attach ourselves to them. When we judge, we open ourselves to picking up their energy and attaching ourselves to what we judged. We can't be scared if we don't believe or attach ourselves to it. We must also put healthy boundaries on ourselves.

Song Reference:
Love Myself **by Hailee Steinfeld**

Healthy Boundaries

Placing healthy boundaries can be a solution to many attachment issues. Boundaries are implemented to maintain control over our emotions, mental limitations, and certain physical aspects in order to protect us from becoming attached. By implementing healthy boundaries, everyone has an option to stay and play or leave. Personal boundaries may be set for highly sensitive discussions that can lead to huge conflicts. When implemented, the sensitive discussion will be off limits and not be discussed. With this solution, both parties need to understand that the area will not be discussed and why. This is at times the best way to deal with detachment. We are limited to controlling many existences in our lives, but one remains for sure: we can control our emotions and choose free will.

Picture This

An aunt and niece are very close and get together for Sunday tea weekly, but lately the niece notices that the aunt keeps bringing up politics resulting in heated arguments. The niece loves her aunt and would like to continue Sunday tea, but doesn't like the heated arguments. So, the following Sunday, she explains to her aunt that, going forward, they will not talk about politics anymore. She explains that the subject is causing too many heated arguments and that she feels uncomfortable. The aunt agrees and decides to stop bringing up politics. In this situation, both parties need to agree on setting these boundaries. If one does not follow set boundaries, it might be time to re-evaluate the relationship.

Less Is Better

Sometimes it is best to not be aware of certain information. Having less information is a negative peace tool, but it allows pre-angels to prevent being attached to drama. When pre-angels become aware of knowledge or gossip about someone or something, they might continuously think about it, want to know more, or want to help, which may lead to attachment to said information. Sometimes avoiding the information is best; what we don't know won't hurt us.

Parents and Detachment

If parents do not teach their children about detachment, when situations such as a parent passing away or a marriage ending occur, these children will be emotionally attached to it. Children may lack the coping skills to deal with the situation, so will instead shadow their parents' attachment behaviors. What we were taught as children is often what our parents were taught as children. Parents will attach themselves to these inherited beliefs, and pass these same beliefs down to their children. As we mature, we need to learn how to discern which of these beliefs are true to our well-being, and create our own belief system. Sometimes the reason why pre-angels attach themselves to objects, other pre-angels, and beliefs is because it makes us feel safe, and we are aware of the end results. Fear, rejection, or the unknown is always lingering if we don't detach ourselves from beliefs that don't serve us.

Only the strong detach themselves from beliefs they were taught as children. We were taught at an early age how to attach to beliefs and understand the rewards and punishment system. We should be teaching children about attachment and detachment. Yes, our children need to learn the do's and don'ts, but at a surface level. We need to explain to our children that everything is temporary at each stage of our lives. Once parents teach their children not to attach themselves to anything, they will not have to teach them to detach.

At times we feel that we are on our own to learn how to detach from these inherited beliefs and the punishment and reward system that we have become accustomed to. To create our identity, we can create our own beliefs by researching at the library, on the internet, asking what other pre-angels believe, and trust our own judgment. A belief system exists that is led with the heart and balanced with the ego. The ego is where we hold attachment, so if we lead more with the heart, then any attachment we have is in loving service to our heart. The hardest thing to do is to let go of control. We created it, and then we can remove it. The ultimate reality is that we all are going to die, so let's make it simpler for us to live and LET GO and enjoy the time we share here.

Teaching Four

If everyone learned about detachment then we would not have any problems in this world, in this current life or when we return. Detachment is the skill of letting go of anything that is holding us back from achieving our purpose and being who we want to be. Once we detach, we will become balanced again. Detachment is a healthy way of living and must be done throughout our lives to maintain a healthy spirit, mind, body, heart and soul.

More About Me

During my childhood years, I became stronger and weaker at the same time. Because the surgeons went through my upper back to get to my heart, I seem to endure a lot of pain in my life especially in the lower back. Because of the constant pain, I missed more school and felt drained most of the time. I saw countless doctors about my back issues, but they had no solutions for treatment, and some were too scared to try anything. Eventually, I gave up listening to doctors and healed myself, with my guardian angel (Fidgal) explaining the teachings over and over again. I finally listened to heal myself. I must say it was the best thing I ever did, and I would not listen to any negative jargon. It took some time but the doctors finally diagnosed scoliosis. The surgery was very difficult. It was like a shock to my tiny body. I believe my body healed itself because of my deep side (spiritual) thinking along with being educated by all the logical doctors. I achieved a balance. At times I still struggle with my back, but I got to know what works and what doesn't work.

From the beginning my mother was always there for me. She made it a point that I would not hear anything that doctors said about me. She placed me outside the door when she talked to the doctors. A protector she was, and that also occurred when I was in school. Throughout my school years in the Catholic education system I felt bullied. My classroom was labeled "Special" which developed an extremely negative connotation. The class was moved four times to four different schools during my elementary school years. By allowing this, the education system subconsciously bullied those who happened to be placed in "Special" Education. For example, our classrooms were labeled LE1, LE2, LE3, which was different than the regular names grade 1, grade 2, etc. It made us stick out and open for ridicule. Even the psychologist bullied me by telling me at an early age that I did not meet the norm of testing results in reading and writing and that my parents would have to take care of me for the rest of my life. I retaliated and asked him who makes the norm. He never answered that question. After I told my mother what the psychologist said, she had a chat with him. He just continued the testing and would tell my mom the results. If he had news to give, he gave it to my mother and the principal and my mom would set me outside the door. When I asked her how I was doing, she just said in her Italian accent voice, "You are doing gooda. Just keep going."

When I wasn't being bullied by the school system, various students bullied me at school. My class was labeled "special", and the kids told me every day how special I was by calling me stupid, loser, dumb and at times excluded me as if "special" was a disease of being stupid and they didn't want to catch it. I think the worst part of being bullied was being excluded. The schools excluded us from certain activities that they deemed we were not intellectually capable of participating in. You could feel the energy of the other students when we were left out. They felt higher and better than me, and it broke my heart each time it happened. Each year, my class would move to a different school, which led my classmates and I to believe that even the schools didn't want us. Being excluded is not something that you can stop feeling at eight to ten years old. When hearing terrible words, you can always cover your ears or walk away. When you're excluded, you have to bear the memories and feel the energy associated with it. I moved school to school so I did not have very many friends. As soon as I made friends, I was moved to another school.

In later years, I learned that there are no normal students, and testing shows nothing but logical results. Besides, how could I concentrate on doing tests and remembering who invented the telephone when I was trying to keep my heaven memories alive in my heart and not get taken away from my parents?

Bullying, I later discovered, is a state of loneliness, and it has nothing to do with me. I learned different strategies to deal with it and understood pre-angels who bullied. This helped me to deal with toxic environments that I endured later in life in the workplace. There is always a reason things occur in our lives; we just need to be open to understanding, seeing and learning from it.

I understand now that the Catholic education system at that time (1981) did not know how to deal with a child who had a near-death experience. They did their best with what they knew at that time. I knew years ago that I did not have a learning disability. I felt that this label was given as an excuse to shut me up and control me. I am a practical learner and in those days did not meet the norm of what the teaching style was and I also had the secret of heaven on my mind. I do believe that everyone learns differently. If a child does not meet the education requirements of the system's set learning style, then he/she is stuck with a label of some kind, such as learning disabled. Inevitably the child takes on the notions of that label. Labels should not be given to anyone for any reason.

Despite the experiences, I would not change anything in my educational years. I took the opportunity that was presented to me and learned from it. It was given to me, and I knew from my heaven days that I needed to understand why I was put in these predicaments. Because of the special education classes, I learned how to present and teach using all teaching methods which has made me an excellent teacher, as well as a Peace and Spiritual Mentor.

CHAPTER 4

Living in the Now

"One will always know, when he is living in the moment"
~ Fidgal

JESUS EXPLAINED THAT THE universe will line everything up in a certain time frame in our life, even if we do not understand it. 'On destiny's time not our time' he would often say. We just need patience to believe in the universe and destiny. Einstein revealed to me that destiny is true but one has to help destiny by choosing the right course of action which is free will. We do not have to understand it; we just need to follow through with what the universe is giving or showing us. When we live in the moment, we can hear the messages and see what the universe is guiding us to achieve. At times we mess it up by choosing a different direction (free will); however the universe will continue to give us the same messages until we act on it.

The universe will provide what we need and know when we are ready to receive it. Unfortunately, we do not always accept what the universe gives us and choose a different course of free will and thus we rearrange the universe's mapped plan. Jesus advised not to plan out the day; be free to allow what the universe gives to play out. Free will was given to us to choose the path that the universe presents to us but we at times do not listen. We seem to take the familiar road as it is safe and convenient. In this chapter, we will explain why it's important to live in the now.

When **"fate"** occurs it's a course of events that appear out of nowhere; in other words it's meant to be. It is different than free will. **Free will** is choices that we make every day and that we can make because of freedom. If we paid attention to what the universe puts in our lives, we wouldn't have to think about or analyze anything. We would just go with the natural flow and follow what the universe provides for us. Usually, if it's natural it is meant to be good; it's pure and simple to see. Simple is a peaceful way of existence. Once we follow the universe, then everything will line up, and we won't have to do much work. We are fortunate to have free will, though at times we mess it up by choosing something totally different from what the universe is trying to give us or show us.

Free Will

We all have a mapped plan, and we change it by our free will. When we live in the now, things will happen and flow, and we won't have to choose. The universe will present various pre-angels, occurrences, money and stuff with divine timing, and then we can use free will to choose whether or not to accept it.

We often make choices that are governed by the logical side. We believe that we are not ready for an opportunity that comes across our path, or we are not living in the moment to see it. We may be afraid of what the opportunity will lead to, so we choose the same route or do nothing. We do not understand why the universe brought this into our lives. Instead of acting out of fear and rejecting the opportunity, we should talk out loud and ask the universe what should be done in the moment. Messages will appear to confirm what the universe would like us to do. Messages are all around us. When not living in the moment we are unable to clearly see what is right in front of us – the golden ticket. Many have golden tickets show up in their lives, and the universe will never give up on showing them. They will continue to appear in our lives as messages. (More detailed information is in the message section of this chapter).

> "It doesn't matter what you believe, it matters to
> see and feel the belief"
> ~ Fidgal

We often do not understand why certain pre-angels or situations appear in our lives and at times, we must be patient to understand the reason. Our logical side is led to analyze things that appear out of nowhere, and we tend to overanalyze. As a result our free will is not so free and we make poor choices. We make many choices throughout our lives that define our current situation. <u>If we do not like the outcome of a choice, we can always choose again</u>. This is our free will. If we keep getting the same results from a choice, it's time to choose again and get a different result. When we are ready for a different result, we will make a different choice. The universe knows what to give us; it feels our feelings, our energy, and reads our thoughts and matches them. It presents the match at divine times in our lives. The key is to see it. Embrace and choose what the universe has displayed; by choosing it, you will find natural bliss. Timing is the key to everything in this dimension and at times we want to see it now. The universe doesn't work that way. Sometimes it plants a seed and takes time for the various pre-angels involved to make it grow. Just because we do not see it, doesn't mean that it will not appear.

Consciousness

A deep side definition of consciousness is living in the now: knowing what is around us, acknowledging our surroundings, living in the moment, a feeling of awareness, and a sense of selfhood (existence). It can also be known as mindfulness. When we live in the now, we are leading more with the heart and becoming a deeper pre-angel.

Consciousness is not a difficult thing to acknowledge; we do this every second of the day. However, some of us are just focusing on getting things completed and are living non-consciously. How do you know that you are living in the now? When pre-angels do not remember events, they were not living in the now at the time of the event. This can occur because they do not want to be there, or they are rushing, or have something else on their mind. When pre-angels forget they start to get restless and frustrated with themselves. Pre-angels should be awake and aware of their surroundings, as in this dimension time travels fast. When you are not living in the now, the logical side is somewhere else, likely in an illusion state. Thinking of the future is an illusion state which takes over the present. Many pre-angels cannot let go of the past; therefore, again the illusion takes over. To be balanced, we must be in the now and only focus on one activity at a time. This is how we continue living in the now of consciousness. <u>When we multitask we are not living in the now.</u> The now is passing us by.

Resetting ourselves to live in the now is necessary to find peace. The best way to reset ourselves is to stop doing the things that we are doing, recognize where we are at this point and start doing one activity at a time.

Here are some other ways of resetting in order to be conscious and living in the now.

Breathing – This is a simple but powerful way of returning to the now. It re-establishes a connection with the atmosphere that we reside in. To breathe properly and fully, remove yourself from what you are doing for a couple of minutes and close your eyes. Slowly take three deep breaths. Focus on your breathing and nothing else. Acknowledge the feelings in your body. Continue doing sets of three breaths for a couple of minutes. Allow your heart rate to come to a slower pace.

Reiki – The power of energy is held everywhere, including our hands. Place both hands on your heart and breathe normally, in and out. Feel your heart rate become slower. When we close our eyes, this can be a form of meditation.

Picture This

Accidents are terrible, but they are also a sign of not living in the now. Oftentimes pre-angels get into car accidents because they are daydreaming, thinking about their past or future, texting, talking on the phone, eating, or intoxicated. If pre-angels were living in the now, accidents could be prevented. When you feel that another driver almost hit you, it is a reminder from the universe to stay focused and live in the moment.

Song Reference:
***Keep Your Eyes Open* by Need to Breath**

Addictions

It is our free will to become addicted to drugs, alcohol, food, etc. and it's our free will to always choose not to. An addiction is an attachment to emotional pain, which is on the deep side. It is important to understand from a deep side view. If someone has an addiction, he/she has a problem hibernating in the deep side so he/she uses a logical solution like drugs or alcohol to mask the pain. Examples of deep sided problems are the inability to let go of the past, forgiveness issues, not accepting current life, past life memories, trauma, anger and affairs. <u>It is important to know that when an addict is using, it is the only time they feel love for themselves and see themselves for who they truly are</u>. Addicts will go back and forth; some will stop drinking and start doing drugs. It is a vicious cycle.

The reason many children of addicts grow up being like their parents, is because they are comfortable taking the same road. They know exactly what is going to happen.

A large number of pre-angels can't deal with feelings or situations so they start using drugs, alcohol, food or other sources relating to the logical side. This is done to get them to a comfort phase called the "**escape stage**". Pre-angels with addictions can't deal with something in their lives so they convince themselves to use what they believe is a coping skill. Drinking, drugs, etc. is not a coping skill, it's an addiction. An addiction is a cover-up for dealing with an issue and it's a temporary fix that does not last. Over time the addict needs to drink more or do more drugs before reaching that escape stage. Then it doesn't last as long so the addict does more to reach that sensible escape feeling. Addicts haven't dealt with deep sided problems, so they use other means to resolve the deep side issues. Addictions only cause more problems in lives. They are a logical quick fix that simply covers or hides the deep sided problem. It's known that depressed pre-angels will have addictions more than non-depressed pre-angels.

Addicts are not living in the now. They want everything to go away so they live in the future to remove the hurt and pain that they have in the current moment. At times, the addict will not see or hear the message that the universe is giving them until they hit rock bottom and are forced to deal with it by losing everything. Alcohol or drugs take over the ability to concentrate on living in the moment and the consequence is that messages become unclear. Unclear and blurred messages leave the addict hallucinating at times. The substance changes their judgment. When this occurs it's called the "**Blockage phase**". Addicts just want to escape but flash backs of the past haunt them and their current life is passing them by.

There are many programs to assist addicts with rehabilitation. Some work and some do not work. To love yourself, you must try many and seek therapies from both sides, deep and logical to return to you. Both therapies should go hand in hand to achieve balance, which will lead to peace. Taking the time to resolve your addiction is the ultimate self-love and belief that you are worth it. It is not an easy task to live here in this learning world, but if you take the necessary steps to get to know who you are and to love yourself unconditionally, you will receive the ultimate goal, peace in your heart. It is important to recognize that recovery is difficult as it changes your consciousness to being conscious every moment of your day. What is difficult about recovery is that now you have to deal with everything and are forced to live in the moment. But you don't have to do it all at once; you can take baby steps. It is important to focus on getting to a peaceful place in life. It doesn't matter how long it takes; it matters that you get there. We focus too much on time. There is plenty of time to get where we're supposed to go and be. We should surround ourselves with pre-angels who love and support and understand us. Pre-angels who have addictions will place boundaries and self-discipline on themselves. They may go to an Alcoholics Anonymous (AA) on a certain day, keep no liquor in their homes, want to be alone, etc. Those who love them will accept these boundaries and embed them in their relationship with the addict.

Medication

We put too much emphasis on medication these days. Many pre-angels are over medicated because they do not meet the norm of society, they want a quick fix, or don't know where else to go for help. Some pre-angels need medication, but if you are not hurting anyone then be free. Be yourself. What we should do is feel free to look for alternative ways to heal ourselves: change our lifestyle, seek an understanding of what is wrong, and find natural solutions. There are so many resources in today's world and we should start using technology or trusted sources (friends, alternative therapies) to find alternative methods of treatment instead of searching for surface stuff and simply relying on medication.

When we take medication we are altering ourselves chemically; we are not authentic. When we choose to add medication to our bodies, we must be aware that we may not see or hear the messages that the universe is putting in front of us. Sometimes medication clouds our judgment and gives side effects. When medication changes our spirit then we are not ourselves and more problems may occur. To love yourself is to take responsibility to fight for your rights and to find alternative ways to heal. Finding a natural way will rarely give side effects and leaves you open to receive messages of assistance.

Let's face it some of us have to take medication. Recognizing that you are on medication and focusing more on living in the now will help to focus your attention on seeing and hearing the messages that the universe is giving you. Do not think that medication alone will resolve any problem; both sided therapies need to be used. If you feel that you must take medication, incorporating some deep sided therapies into your lifestyle will help you to resolve the problem effectively. Sometimes medication is necessary but we don't need only the logical solutions; we also need the deep solutions to obtain balance and that will give us peace.

Messages

We get messages all the time from the universe, even if we do not see them or feel them. Many of us lead with the want approach and ignore the messages that are right in front of us. At times, we see what we want to see, and use free will to choose what we want which is different from what the message is showing us.

At times we ignore the messages and try to force events to manifest; we try, and compromise our life just to get what we want. Unfortunately, acting based on wants will not make us happy and in time we will have a broken heart or a crisis of spirit. We must acknowledge the "needs" and listen to the messages that the universe is giving us. It is important to know that the universe protects us and gives us messages to help us choose the better path. Messages can come from friends/strangers, a gut feeling, images, body language, television programs, repeating numbers (example: 222, 12:12), and hearing the same quotes over and over again, etc. Sometimes the messages are not for us; they are for someone that we connect with. We must deliver these messages to others. Be conscious of these messages, acknowledge them and follow what they are telling us, especially when the universe keeps giving us the same results and the same messages over and over. We are just too stubborn to listen, and instead of acting on it we praise the ego and ignore the messages.

Picture This

A man and woman are dating. Each is into the other, but the woman is more into the relationship than the man. They date for five years, during which the woman keeps having a gut feeling that something is not right in this relationship. Her boyfriend continuously seems to disappear, and she hears the same song on the radio: "Ghost" by Fefe Dobson. She ignores the messages and marries him anyway. After their second child is born, she finds out that her husband has been cheating on her since day one. When we force manifesting and start messing with divine timing, we get unnatural results which will hurt us down the road. We must trust in the messages and listen to our intuition. The universe loves us unconditionally, is always protecting us, and will provide everything in divine timing.

—

The universe knows what is best; it has gotten you this far. The good news is that it will keep showing things and/or pre-angels in your life. When you see the same pre-angel over and over again, it means that the universe would like you to have a relationship with that pre-angel, either as a friend or lover. The universe has planted the seed. Now you, as part of the universe, allow the seed to grow by thinking of the pre-angel over and over or hanging around them.

So, if you miss a message, the universe will continue to put it in your path again and again until you see it and follow through with it. The messages can come through thoughts of someone, quotes, a song, a feeling that keeps coming up and even a vision in your dreams. We all have a beginning (birth) and an ending (death), but it is what's in between that truly defines life. We always end up at the exact ending that the universe wants us to, even with free will.

Teaching Five

Destiny's time not our time! We need patience to believe in the universe by choosing the right course of free will. We do not have to understand it; we just need to follow through with what the universe is giving us. Messages are guiding us to achieve. At times though, we mess it up by choosing a different path. The universe, however, will continue to give us the same message until we act on it.

CHAPTER 5

The Universe

*"Our lives are changing, and we have to
catch up to what the universe wants us to change"*
~ Fidgal

Seven Senses

FIRST IMPRESSIONS ARE VERY important in today's world.
Everyone has met someone new in their lifetime. When
you meet someone new do you ever notice their energy
and how it feels to you?

In this learning world, we have senses that have
been created within our bodies. Most of us have been
blessed with five senses and use them often in our daily
lives. The five commonly known senses are sound,
sight, touch, smell, and taste. While I was visiting
heaven, I had a fantastic visit with Einstein who explained about two other unrecognized senses that are
very powerful in our dimension. They are Intuitive En-

ergy and the Environment. We already know and understand the five basic senses, so I will explain why the two added senses are so important in our life.

First, let's make sure that we understand what this profound expression "Intuitive Energy" means, from what I learned in heaven. Intuitive energy is without rational thought, or thinking with the mind. It can be as strong as all the senses put together, a combination of all the senses intertwined into one instant. This energy is hidden, not visible to the other senses like the human eye. It is an invisible sense that can help everyone to understand others. It must start with trusting your intuition. Is the energy you feel positive or negative? This is the key to using this invisible sense. Believe what you imagine, trust how you feel, trust the vibration, trust what you hear, trust the environment around you, trust the taste that you are experiencing, and trust the smell that's around you. In combinations, you have invisible vibrational energy, Intuitive Energy.

The Environment can project a cold or warm comfortable feeling. It portrays an important sense for leading you to a conclusive feeling. We should question what type of environment or atmosphere we are involved in or are located in. A sense of what type of environment is displayed or felt. Are we in a safe place? The environment feeling can be misdirected by where we are in our current life situation. If the walls are dark and untouched, then our life may be dark and unhappy. We should set-up our environment to show where we want to be now. We can use light colors or bright colors, something creative, and display visions of positive messages to create a happier environment. With any situation the environment can tell so much of where pre-angels are in their lives.

Teaching Six

Invisible Vibrational Energy is the most profound sense that is overlooked and not even acknowledged. This invisible feeling of energy is also called "intuitive energy." It builds up our trust factor and is always around us. We should trust our intuition.

Life is like a Movie

Both Jesus and Einstein were adamant in explaining that many in the future will not live in the now because of technology and other factors. They will create challenges in their lives that are not necessary. In heaven everyone works together as one. As the saying goes, "as it is in heaven" so we should do the same on earth. Competition has taken over our lives and pre-angels want the whole pie. Both mentors taught me that there is enough to go around and we should take a piece of the pie instead of the whole pie. When we want the whole pie we allow the ego to take over. No one wins when the ego takes over. We were taught to share at an early age in grade school but we seem to be missing that teaching when we get older. The older we get the more conditioned we are to lead with the logical side. Einstein always said to me that succeeding alone is an unknown factor, one that does not exist.

Some pre-angels think that they are alone in this world. There is no one to assist or serve us and no one for us to assist and serve. Being alone is another illusion that we need to address. To understand this concept, Einstein explained to me that our lives are like a movie. When we watch a movie, the credits show that it's a team that created it.

Picture This

Support is shown when a team of pre-angels come together to achieve one goal. A movie is created like this with expertise. There is so much more to a movie than the famous leading actors. It takes an entire team to put together a feature film, sometimes thousands of pre-angels. Expertise is needed from many sources: writers, camera operators, those who repair cameras, producers, directors, gaffers and caterers for food to name just a few. At the end of the movie, a long list of credits and recognition are given to all the pre-angels that helped support the movie production. All are involved with a common end goal – a story in pictures, a movie.

This concept can be applied to life: it is just like creating a movie. We all need help to live our lives and achieve the plot (purpose). In the end, we are going to get the same conclusion, which is death. Depending on what you believe, we have a team in heaven and the universe working for us, and we should have a team down here. That's why we have family and friends. We are all part of each other's stories. We need to remove the competitiveness, which is ego driven, and the want attitude. There is enough money, love, fame and knowledge for everyone to share. There is enough money to go around in the world, and if not, more can be printed. We are here to make a difference in each other's lives. We are here to help each other, not compete. Give value to your friends and loved ones, and you will receive it back from the universe.

Song Reference:
Stand By You **by Rachel Platten**

Teaching Seven

It is critical to understand that we are never alone in this world. No one will succeed without others, plus, we always have the universe helping us to achieve greatness. We are not alone, and should work as a team to resolve issues and to achieve our purpose. We need to remove the competitiveness as there is enough to go around.

Soul Recognition

Have you ever met someone, felt as if you have known them for years and carried on a deep conversation during the first meeting? You can talk for hours and not even notice how much time has gone by. This pre-angel is from your soul family. With **soul recognition** the soul already knows them, but from the logical side we do not realize who they are or how we know them. Soul recognition is often referred to as kindred spirit. All of us will meet our soul family, whether we are conscious of it or not. Our soul family was with us in heaven before we chose our purpose to come here. These souls have been with us before our life paths, again and again in past lives. When we are with a member of our soul family, we are at the highest vibrational energy, beyond what is here in this world; an energy otherwise only known to angels in heaven.

When we meet a member of our soul family, we feel complete trust and love. We disclose our deepest thoughts and feelings without even knowing the pre-angel. Their vibration matches our feelings, and they do not have to tell us what they are going through because we can feel it. We feel safe, happy, and confident that we can tell them anything and it won't offend them. We are drawn to them like a magnet. They will never judge us or give up on us, and will always be willing to help. Ego is always removed when we are with a member of our soul family. We always are there for them when they need help or just want to talk. They will stay with us forever in all dimensions; we don't have to be with them every minute of the day to feel their presence. Once we meet a member of our soul family, it is critical to connect with them. They know us best and can guide us in achieving our purpose and help us to find peace. We should always talk and connect with them throughout our lives, as they have been there from the beginning of time with us. The universe knows of our soul family and will reunite us in divine timing.

Vibrational Intimacy

Many of us have had the pleasure of being in love, the feeling of great peace and a burst of energy that resonates through us. Love is the ultimate feeling in this world. Or is it? When we meet members of our soul family, one of them is our soul mate. There is another ultimate feeling that surpasses love, and that is Vibrational Intimacy. **Vibrational Intimacy** is a powerful feeling that we will never feel in ordinary circumstances, until we meet our soul mate. It's a connection of souls resulting in a burst of energy that vibrates throughout our bodies. It's a feeling of trust, understanding, deep connection, confidence, love, and intimacy. It's a happy heart feeling, like you feel when giving your time to help others. It's like the after effects of an orgasm, except it lasts for days. Soul mates can feel the energy of each other. They know their partner's needs, how to handle problems with them, and they connect on a deeper level of consciousness. Soul mates talk easily to each other about anything and stay silent for hours on a deeper level just holding each other, an intimate level that is beyond love and sex combined. Vibrational intimacy is like making love effortlessly. Messages from the universe are stronger than ever when you have vibrational intimacy. Soul mates can learn a lot from each other. When you find your soul mate, you will be in the zone, frozen in time with no one around you but him/her. You will know each other's feelings and be able to give messages beyond verbal communication. It's a feeling of love, consciousness, intimacy, leading with the heart and heaven all wrapped up in one feeling. Vibrational Intimacy is what heaven feels like. We will all experience vibrational intimacy in our lives; we just need to be open to it.

With divine timing (right place at the right time), the man/ woman of your dreams will appear, and everyone around you will become invisible. When you reach this vibrational intimacy, it is the most profound level of consciousness that you will have. This vibration will leave you speechless and make you want to connect with your soul mate more. It changes the way you see things. Everything is beautiful, especially while you are with your soul mate. You think of them often while you are apart. After connecting with your soul mate and achieving this vibrational intimacy, the vibration will continue to radiate even after you've said bye. Some would call this love, but it's beyond love; it's unconditional love. Every pre-angel has a soul mate that they hope to bond with as one. When we find our soul mate and soul family, we should embrace them, as they are the closest that we will get to understand ourselves.

Picture This

A young woman was returning with her parents from Arizona to Detroit. When checking in at the airport, her mother requested seats on the plane for the three of them together. The airline attendant managed to put the parents together but could not change the young woman's seat. The attendant apologized and explained that each time she attempted to change the seat the computer system would move it back to the original seat, 24A. She tried three times. The young woman accepted the seat and was happy to have a seat as the flight was full. The next thing she knew, a man sat next to her. The woman struck up a conversation.

"Wow, do you ever look like David Foster!" fell from her lips.

"Who's that?" the man answered.

"Never mind. He is Canadian."

"I am Canadian too."

The young woman felt that she had known this man for years. She noticed a deepness to him when he spoke. He was intrigued when she introduced him to the law of attraction, the ability to attract what you want and need in your life by focusing on positive thoughts and feelings. They talked throughout the entire flight about the personal challenges they had faced and the heartache they both endured. The man was having a crisis of spirit and needed some valuable guidance. The young woman gave messages to him about letting go and finding out who he wants to be now. They both knew subconsciously what messages they had to give to each other. The man asked where the woman worked. When she explained that she would be starting at a foot clinic he had a confused look on his face and expressed that he did not see her at a foot clinic. He asked her point blank, "What do YOU really want to do"?

She was shocked and answered bravely, "I always wanted to write self-help books and be a motivational speaker."

"So why don't you just do that?" he asked. It felt like time was frozen around them.

After the flight, the man gave his business card to the young woman and helped her with her bags. As he walked away, he turned back to see her one last time.

⁓

In many cases the universe plants a seed for us to see and lets it go to see if it grows. If it doesn't grow, then the universe will again present it perhaps in a different way to attract our attention. The man on the plane and the young woman were put on that flight at the right time and right place (divine timing) for one purpose: to meet. They needed to hear the messages of moving forward; her with a career change and him with his personal life. The young woman felt that she knew the man on the plane for years because she probably had. They were from the same soul family.

There are many instances that the universe displays and will continue to until we realize that it's meant to be. The universe knows exactly what we need at certain time frames in our lives and will present it to us. It will match our feelings and thoughts with what we need. Sometimes we do not see or want to believe what the universe puts in front of us because we feel we are not ready or we are not living in the moment to see it. Often times we use free will to choose to mess it all up. Messages will continue to come back again and again until we wake up and notice them. It doesn't matter how long it takes to understand the messages and follow through. It matters that we get there.

The universe planned this meeting, and it's called "fate". What you didn't know was that the man on the plane booked his flight one day before, and there was only one seat available: the seat beside the young woman. If that is not fate then what is? Coincidences are created by the universe for a reason. If we just follow what the universe presents to us then we would go with the flow and live a happier life and not question it. When the universe is being questioned it is the ego doing the questioning. The universe knows us better than we know ourselves. The universe is always creating the perfect message to give us.

Coincidences

A **coincidence** is an extraordinary concurrence of events or circumstances that just occur out of nowhere. It is supernatural, the universe working together to plan our destiny. Coincidences occur for various reasons that are unknown to us. There is always a reason why pre-angels show up in our lives. The best way to understand them is to acknowledge and follow what the universe shows you. If you keep bumping into someone, talk to them and get to the know them. The universe has placed them in your life for a reason. We need to investigate the reason as the universe can only plant a seed. The rest is up to us to achieve.

CHAPTER 6

Relationships

*"The slowest development of a relationship
builds a sustainable relationship"*
~ Fidgal

EINSTEIN DIDN'T SAY MUCH about relationships, mainly focusing on the energy of pre-angels in relationships. Jesus and Fidgal guided me more on relationships. I recall that when I spoke to Jesus about relationships Einstein would smile and say "Yes, that sounds right." Then Einstein would start telling me a logical story ending with a deep sided message. He did say that he took too long to let go of pre-angels and other sources in his life. He never said it black or white though; there was always an understanding that you had to realize with his teachings. Einstein spoke more about letting go and exploring different roads. Jesus was more understanding of relationships, speaking of loving everyone including yourself.

The key to understanding our relationships is to understand ourselves first. Loving ourselves is the primary objective to being happy in this world. Once we love ourselves, we will know who we are, and choose the ideal relationship for us. To love ourselves we need to realize our wants and needs. We have to unconditionally accept our mind, body, spirit and soul to truly know how to love another pre-angel. A relationship will not make you happy; you need to love yourself and make yourself happy first. When we love ourselves, the ego dies. Happiness goes hand-in-hand with loving ourselves. When we understand ourselves, we can begin to understand what we can give to a relationship to enhance our happiness.

Realizing our needs and wants, and what we can give to others, will help us succeed in every type of relationship. Without this understanding, we will not be able to select the right partner for a meaningful relationship or find our soul mate. Once we learn to love ourselves then the universe will deliver the right partner. Remember, our wants are temporary desires and our needs are long lasting. Most of today's relationships have become about our personal wants; we do not consider our needs. We should ask ourselves what our needs are. When our wants (logical) become more important than our needs (deep) we become imbalanced, and the relationship will develop turmoil. Throughout the years we have lost the ability to honor ourselves. When we honor ourselves by loving ourselves and putting ourselves first we can truly accept our partner in the same loving way. Loving ourselves first results in many more happy and fulfilling relationships and far fewer divorces.

Part of having a successful relationship is recognizing the dynamics of our relationships. Every relationship needs positive invisible vibrational energy as when it started, as well as communication, to succeed. Talking about money, kid's events, material possessions and surface stuff is not real communicating. When in relationships, we should never stop dating our partner. When you love yourself, 'me time' is like dating yourself. The same concept applies to relationships with two pre-angels. Spending time with each other is how the communication continues, and the invisible vibrational energy stays in play.

Make time to be with each other, and if it doesn't work out then maybe it's time to re-evaluate the relationship. When we don't make time for each other, we are not truly committed to either ourselves or our partner. Sometimes, in a relationship we need to compromise and keep our comments to ourselves to avoid a conflict. Small things that are not worth getting upset about come up. To keep the peace, some self-discipline is required. When we approach a relationship superficially, we get superficial results. We convince ourselves that we put effect into relationships, but in most cases all we are doing is "trying" to work on them. Trying is a weak, ego-minded approach, not dealing with core issues in the relationships and ourselves. It is a token effort when we are unwilling to make the commitment to lead with our hearts. If all we ever do is scratch the surface of our relationships, we never truly know if it was meant to be.

There is a saying we must understand that the quickest relationships dissolves as fast as you get them. The more we spend time and live in the moment with our partner, the more the relationship will sustain itself and we will get to know them better each time.

Teaching Eight

In any relationship we have, communication is primary. So many times couples break up because one is not honest with themselves or their partner. Truth is harder than a lie and we forget the lie at times. To understand anyone, we must be honest. When you are honest and communicate that way, it will set you free. No one knows what you are thinking.

⁓

We will have many different relationships in our lives: the romantic relationship, family and friend relationships, and the relationships with ourselves. In this chapter, we will be focusing on the romantic relationship, but many of the ideas can be used in any relationship that you are involved in.

Within romantic relationships there are four distinct dynamics that are most often encountered. They are the Shifting Relationships, Interdependent Relationships, Guilt Relationships, and True Relationships. Realizing the type of relationship that we are involved in can help us better understand how to contribute to its success or decide to end it. Another significant factor to discuss is how the invisible vibrational energy of your partner factors in starting, continuing or ending the relationship.

Shifting Relationship

In a shifting relationship, two pre-angels come together at the same invisible vibrational energy. When this type of relationship begins to fail, it is because one pre-angel is growing, meaning their invisible vibration energy has changed, and the other stays the same. They are no longer in sync. This is the main reason a **shifting relationship** starts crumbling; one pre-angel is shifting to a higher consciousness while the other partner, the "non-shifter," is holding on to the past superficiality, and staying in his/her comfort zone.

Over the years, so many relationships fail when there is a detachment from love. This happens because we lose ourselves in the relationship and start putting logical activities, money, home, and friends first before our self-love. At the beginning of a romantic relationship, the honeymoon stage which lasts 1 to 3 years, everything is amazingly thrilling until one partner begins to shift to a higher invisible vibrational energy. Many logical sided couples' relationships become this way. Between the 7th to 12th years, the invisible vibrational energy starts to change within the relationship. This is called "**transitional love**", and many couples continue their relationships this way. With transitional love, problems develop, leaving one partner vibrating at a different energy level than the other. They feel unfulfilled and often experience a crisis of spirit. This is where they begin to overanalyze their relationship and themselves. They experience unhappiness, depression, regret, and odd behaviors may begin to surface. One partner will feel that the other is draining their energy and they can feel quite tired. One logical pre-angel and one deep pre-angel are like oil and water when they are not connecting. This does not mean that they cannot be successful in a relationship; it just means real effort and a lot of changes will be required by both. Transitional love does not occur with soul mates.

The solution to every relationship is communication, communication! Communicating means spending time with each other, talking about needs and wants, and using the deep side to express emotions. Communication is not all about talking; it's also about listening to a partner's needs and wants. If a relationship has gone too long without communication, then non-loving behavior and distance will occur between the partners. Without communication, intimacy no longer exists and is replaced with surface talk or actions. Complaining, non-coping behaviors, avoidance and control issues appear. Affairs and online romantic involvements can begin to fill the need for intimacy. When these behaviors occur, the love is fading, and the energy is being drained from the relationship.

Avoidance is a big behavior displayed when love is gone. Avoidance is used to give the other pre-angel the sword to end the relationship. Usually the one who is shifting or needs more will be invited to end the relationship. Often the non-shifter who is doing the avoidance doesn't want to take that responsibility, so they wait until the other partner decides to let go. The non-shifter has designed their life so that they do not have to take any risks and live vicariously through the other partner.

It is important to understand that logical pre-angels can only handle so much interaction with deep pre-angels. With this type of relationship logical pre-angels prefer small talk, are independent and generally just want to get things done and over with. Deep pre-angels, on the other hand feel the need to share their feelings, be compassionate and spread love. They are forever hopeful that they can change their partner into being a deeper pre-angel. Deep pre-angels at times feel curtailed by the logical pre-angel's approach to getting ahead in the world by using money. One of the most incredible and golden keys to any relationship is allowing growth and change. If you don't grow in a relationship or accept growth in your partner, then self-righteousness and unhappiness will take over. In the end conflicting issues will arise and love of yourself will disappear.

"If we do not allow our loved one to change and grow,
then we run the risk of destroying them"
~ Fidgal

With a shifting relationship, if one is not growing, then the relationship will not last. It becomes stagnant and non-coping skills in managing the relationship will appear. Managing the relationship can cause a great deal of stress and heartache. If one cannot be themselves, then nothing matters. If conflicts arise trust is gone, and it may be time to learn from the relationship, move on and start exploring the relationship with ourselves again.

Interdependent Relationship

Can one logical pre-angel and one deep pre-angel continue to have a lasting relationship? The answer is yes; love can conquer all. An **Interdependent Relationship** is a loving relationship that is built on living separate lives according to the individuals' invisible vibrational energy, lifestyle and beliefs. If they can accept each other's energies, trust each other and communicate their feelings and beliefs, they can enjoy a lasting and meaningful relationship. Open communication, honesty, and trust will dominate this type of relationship. Logical pre-angels at times may not understand deep pre-angels and vice versa; the language can be foreign. But a simple explanation of each other's beliefs can resolve unknown conflicts. The deep pre-angel will seek other deep pre-angels' friendship, send love, be affectionate, give to charity and help their communities. They have a deep desire to explore their existence and understand the meaning of life. The logical pre-angel will be geared to more "want" based activities to meet their expectations, including hanging out with logical friends and spending money. Both have to accept each other's beliefs and lifestyles if they want to continue in the relationship. In any relationship communication is a must but with this relationship it is even more important. Communication builds trust and is the deal breaker. Both partners must develop good listening skills, compromise, spend time with each other, attend various surface/deep pre-angels events and be independent. This type of relationship can be more challenging at times, but also more rewarding. It is always being refreshed with new learning experiences, new adventures, and always achieving balance. This relationship requires constant open-mindedness and communication, or it will disintegrate to a more shifting relationship.

There are distinct differences between the shifting and interdependent relationship. In the interdependent relationship, both parties are aware of and accept the partners' different beliefs and lifestyles, and they choose to live separate lives. They love each other deeply and want to make the relationship successful. The interdependent relationship is based on the theory that opposites attract. In a shifting relationship, couples start off at the same invisible vibrational energy, then one starts shifting and love fades away. In both relationships, we can find ourselves thinking that the other has attributes of both, and so using the peace tool of communication to continue the relationship is ideal. However, if communication and fighting occur, pursuing these two types of relationships is forcing it, and forcing leads to nothing but the same results. <u>It is important to understand that when the universe gives you the same results it is an indication that the universe is protecting you by telling you to move on</u>. Many feel that they are alone in these types of relationships.

In any relationship, we want our partner to grow, and, at times, suggest various ways that we think they can grow. We must understand that when our partner is ready to make the change it will come naturally. If we force someone to change, then the change will be artificial, and will not last in the relationship. Pre-angels change because they want to change, not because you gave them an ultimatum to change. We must honor their timing of change.

Guilt Relationship

A **Guilt Relationship**, also known as an "unrealistic" relationship is based on convenience and the logical side (ego). This relationship is guided by the "want approach". Many couples remain in guilt relationships because of their children or other logical matters such as money and material possessions. In this type of relationship, the pre-angel feels they are just running through the motions, not living in the now. Guilt relationships are based on decisions of the "wants" and staying "in the comfort zone". Partners refuse to allow the relationship to end because they want everything their way. Some inappropriate behaviors will manifest in guilt relationships, including one or both partners being controlling, angry, self-sabotaging, managing and passive/aggressive. Infidelity is more likely to occur in guilt relationships. .

Sometimes, pre-angels stay together because they don't want their partner to get half of the money or material possessions. Living with someone because you don't want to separate assets is an ego solution. Ego solutions never work in the long run. Money and material possessions can always be replaced. Happiness and freedom cannot be replaced or bought. If you want to enjoy money and material possessions, do it on your terms and with someone who can enjoy those things with you, or do it alone. When we put money before life, we are saying our life is worth a bunch of numbers. Money in this world is worth nothing. We cannot go to the doctor and say we want a new life, nor can we bring our money with us when we die. We can only enjoy the life we have now. In the end, material possessions will be split, and you wasted all that time worrying and holding on to money for nothing. Sharing money with your partner grudgingly and being unable to use your money freely is like going back to live under your parents' roof as a teenager and asking for money every time you want to use it.

At other times a partner in a relationship will compromise just to get through everyday life. We need to compromise, but if it takes over our lives happiness is gone and only bitterness remains in our hearts. Compromise should not be leading a relationship; love should. Too much compromising develops into negative energy that vibrates inside the home. When we continuously have to compromise, and love is fading away, it's time to move on and see what else the universe has in store for us.

"You can never replace time,
you can always replace money"
~ Fidgal

Many parents stay in guilt relationships for their children. Children are smarter than we give them credit for. Staying in a guilt relationship because of children is like surviving on the Titanic. No one wins; scars and invisible bitterness stay within the children's minds and hearts. Parents should know that their children have higher intuition than they do, and can feel the fakeness that lies between their parents. It is seen many times over and over again that after children leave for college the parents' relationship ends. Couples who split up at this time wasted many years in an unhappy relationship simply because they did not love themselves enough to let go of their partner. Their children's energy can change to match their own during this time of denial. So, if the parent is upset, the child will match that energy and unexplained behaviors may appear. Children will be left with an unknown bitterness that they will not be able to understand in adulthood.

The best thing that parents can do is to teach their children about detachment and show them that they love themselves enough to put themselves first. When we continue in a guilt relationship, conflicts will occur. The results will continue to be logical (ego) which leads to emptiness in the end. Loving ourselves is the ultimate way of detachment.

Staying in a relationship because you want to save your partner is another form of guilt relationship. Do you love them or do you want to save them? It takes a lot of courage to stay in a guilt relationship because you want to save your partner. You can help them, but you don't have to take their abuse because of their addictions, mental illness or sickness either. Sometimes you have to love them and not complain and accept things in order to keep the peace during this time in the relationship. A lot of patience and compassion is needed to care for someone who is sick. Pre-angels who stay in this type of relationship feel guilty for living their life freely if they leave. We all should give compassion, but if the compassion becomes empathy, then we will lose ourselves in the relationship. If we love someone, we accept them for who they are. This can sometimes be confused with saving them. No one can save anyone; a pre-angel can only save themselves. Once we start doing everything for them, we start losing ourselves and not putting ourselves first. Over time we will start feeling resentful and angry and usually depression follows. If you want to save them, start living your life. Attend support groups. Do things for you. Help them, but know the difference between helping them and saving them, and set boundaries on when to help. Save your spirit, or it will be taken away. It is difficult to care for pre-angels who are sick, but one should do it with good intentions. When pre-angels are sick and close to dying, it is difficult for the loved one to accept. They should get assistance and live their life also; that's why there are professional organizations to assist and give you some release time. If the loved one doesn't want to use these services, then they are being selfish and leading with their ego. We can help each other, but when we lose ourselves we become sick too. Give your worries to the universe, ask for assistance using the law of attraction, and do research to find services in your area. Allow your energy and understanding to let go of the empathy.

To conclude, life is precious and can be taken away at any moment. Our life means more than the accumulation of our wants. If our relationship is fading and we have done everything to achieve balance, then it is time to let go, learn from it and move on. We need to be honest with ourselves and love ourselves enough to move on, detach and put ourselves first. Through putting ourselves first, we give our children the gift of being able to let go. With any guilt relationship, we must be true to ourselves and save ourselves.

Picture This

Imagine that you are in a beautiful valley. The sun is shining bright, the birds are chirping, and the grass is a vibrant green. You are climbing a large hill heading up from the valley. Down at the bottom on the other side of the hill is your soul mate. He or she is sitting beside a lovely pond on a red and white checker cloth waiting for you to join him/her. When you get to the top of the hill, though, there is a chain across your path. In front of the

T

chain is your current partner, stopping you from going down the hill to the other side where your soul mate waits. The universe can only do so much for you. Free will is yours. If you stay on top of the hill, you will receive the same results with your current partner. Sometimes we have to learn to let go of the pre-angels we think we want in order to grow and find the love that we need to shine. We must learn from the relationships, renew ourselves with love, and re-explore our wants and needs again. To love yourself is to move past the current partner, remove the chain, go down the hill and see what the universe is offering.

"Sometimes you have to let go of the one person who is holding you back from being who you want to be".
~ Fidgal

Song Reference:
Good Goodbye **by Diana DeGarmo**

Teaching Nine

When something in our lives is rough and unpleasant, we must learn from it and let it go. Holding on to someone who is not allowing growth is holding us back from the next chapter in our lives that the universe has set up. To let go is the hardest thing to do, but the strongest way that you can show love for yourself.

True Relationship

A **True Relationship** is the most fulfilling one. It's authentic because each pre-angel vibrates at the same energy level and it is continuous. It is the most loving and fulfilling relationship and what everyone is seeking in this world. In this relationship, we just intuitively know exactly what our partner needs and wants. The invisible vibrational energy can be very powerful in an authentic relationship; love is continuous and pure. Love and affection flow effortlessly. Even in a true relationship obstacles will arise. However, when this happens in a true relationship the connection becomes even stronger; love and support will shine even more. This is the golden relationship that is natural, honest and trusting, with everlasting vibrational intimacy flowing. It has the ultimate balance between the "wants" logical side of sex and the "needs" deep side of intimacy. To find a true relationship, we must learn to love ourselves unconditionally. We should never accept anything less for ourselves. Just like in heaven, life will glide and flow until everything fits just right.

Song Reference:
***Atmosphere* by Andy Chrisman**

Workaholics

A **workaholic** is a pre-angel who focuses only on work and work alone. Workaholics are mainly logical pre-angels with logical jobs. These are pre-angels who focus all their time and energy on the logical side because they are avoiding something in their lives. For example, let's say a husband is a workaholic and the wife looks after the family. Because the workaholic is not available, the wife feels rejected causing her to find an attachment to something else such as their children or material possessions. We make sacrifices, but if we put the logical side before our family, then we will receive logical results. When the husband comes home, the wife may reject him because she has felt so much rejection herself. The wife adopts the same rejection energy of the husband. The husband then attaches himself to working even more, feeling that he can control work better than his marriage.

When there is an imbalance in the relationship and no one is dealing with it, the energy builds up until a crisis of spirit appears. A job is to help you survive in this world. But when a job takes over the relationship with yourselves or your family, then you have given up on the deep side, which is love. While you may think of working as showing love, your family feels that you are avoiding them and work is more important than they are.

When rejection is constantly endured in a marriage, the partner may feel attached to empty memories. An attachment of absence, of not being there, may appear. They cannot let go of the constant rejection that they have felt, sometimes for years. A broken heart one or two times is very different from years of rejection. When pre-angels hold on to empty memories, it's hard to recover.

There comes a point when that workaholic husband wants to return to the family and spend time with them. He takes time off of work hoping that it makes up for past absences, incorrectly believing he can regain those memories. The wife by then may have attachment to previous empty promises, so she thinks that as soon as he returns to work, the cycle will continue. She fears him making more empty memories again. The trust factor is gone due to the fear of broken promises. The wife has become accustomed to being left alone and now feels more comfortable in that state. Therefore, she may not want him to take time off and attempt to return.

In today's market, job security is hard to come by even with union agreements and contracts. A job situation can change at any time, a job can be lost, or a career change is required. This can cause a workaholic to have a crisis, for their world is turned upside down. They feel out of place with their family as well as in their career. Usually, the workaholic wants to change when they experience a crisis or an illness in the family. Until that time comes, they will continue to do what they know: working. Working is a safe place, a place where they can lead and results appear to them. Over time, the workaholic may experience a crisis of spirit, develop regrets and try to change his/her ways, but it might be too late. While every relationship is different, it may be difficult for a partner to forgive constant rejection.

Parents/Mothers

Many parents hold the whole world on their shoulders. This could be either the mother or the father. Typically and traditionally it was the mother who took on the major caretaker role, but in modern times fathers do this as well. For convenience in explaining this section, the term mother will be used as an *example*. When a woman becomes a mother, she becomes a different pre-angel; a shift into the caretaker role takes over. This can be a fantastic time for a woman, but also a shifting time. Many mothers create an invisible bubble around themselves and their children. They attach themselves totally to taking care of the children, which can lead to losing themselves, and the attraction that drew them to their partner slowly disappears. At times, they are so busy multitasking, that they stop taking care of themselves and stop living in the moment. They gain weight, wear lazy clothes, stop communicating with their partner, and let their own health fail. They lose themselves, and the husbands fall out of love with them. The mother loses herself, becomes someone who she does not understand and wonders how she got to this place.

The invisible vibrational energy changes in the relationship when one becomes a mother. At times, subconsciously, a mother will start acting older and more caring behaviors will surface. She may worry, make unnecessary noises in her sleep, snore, rushes, and not pay attention to her husband or herself. A mother can easily lose interest in her husband and pay more attention to their children. Mothers need to understand that children are with them temporarily and must practice letting them go as they will go off to college and eventually start their own families. Many fathers need to take on more responsibilities by helping out with the children, giving the mother a break. This will increase the invisible vibrational energy in the home and help with reconnecting and staying connected as a couple.

A mother's responsibility is to teach her children about love, being responsible and living. If a mother is not doing this herself, what kind of example is she providing? When you attach yourself to one entity and the entity leaves, you will be left with a broken heart. The solution for anyone who has lost themselves in a relationship is to take back yourself. The key is to strive for balance by taking care of yourself, having me time and connecting with your partner/spouse.

It is known that when the children go to college, a substantial number of mothers feel alone. The logical term "empty nest syndrome" kicks in. If she did not continue to connect with her husband, and lost sight of herself, a crisis of spirit will develop. At this time a mother may attach herself to other things like shopping, or acting like they are single in order to feel important again. She may even require more sex from her husband. Every relationship is different, but if a mother has cared for her children and lost sight of herself, she will start creating another attachment when the children are gone. She is looking for something logical to mask what is missing in her life, while what she is really missing is love for herself. Couples become comfortable with avoiding each other, as they have lost themselves in the relationship and at times do not even like each other. A crisis of spirit can overtake the pre-angel's world.

With any relationship, it starts with you! When you lose yourself, you lose everything around you and inside of you too. So, find out who you want to be now. When either partner loses himself/herself, the other partner is likely to lose interest. The priority is to never lose yourself in any relationship. *Loving yourself is the solution to everything in your life.*

After the Children

Once a couple has children, a lot of the conversation is directed towards the home front, and over time the communication becomes stale. Children are a blessing, a bond between two pre-angels. When a couple's relationship is all focused on the children, it loses the invisible vibrational energy between the couple. That's why it is essential to never stop dating and getting to know your partner. Couples should schedule couple time every week. Penning is permanent, penciling is temporary. Life can get busy, but we all have choices to make, and we choose to stay busy, so go back to the beginning where the invisible vibrational energy was at the highest peak and stay there.

Single

Single is great, and one should enjoy time as a single pre-angel. When we are single, we have the opportunity to do what we want and find out who we truly are. For most pre-angels there comes a time when a loving relationship with another is needed to grow.

If we choose not to be single we must connect with that one pre-angel out of seven billion on earth. This can take what feels like an eternity for some. At weddings, some single pre-angels can feel as if the universe forgot about 'their' one. They get discouraged, and tired of waiting for the one. A crisis of waiting can occur. They wonder when the one is going to come along, cry for no reason, talk to themselves when they meet someone or ask "What's wrong with me?" When they meet someone they ask, "Is he or she the one?" This crisis of waiting can shake the trust that the one is out there. During these shaking times, we must strive for balance and believe that it will happen. Patience, patience, and if it is meant to be the universe will send the perfect pre-angel on their time, not on our time. Show the universe that you are ready: be good to yourself, be open to anything that comes your way and focus on the now. Patience, patience is the key. Love yourself first and be open to allow someone to love you too.

Pre-angels say that you will find the one when you least expect it. From a deep side of this statement, that's because the universe knows exactly the right time, the right place to present the right pre-angel on our path. The question is: will you allow them to share your life, or choose to stay in your single world? We do our best to stay busy, and it shows the universe that we are not available to find love. We should invest more in living and less in material possessions. Sometimes we design our lives so that we don't have to take any risks and live vicariously through other pre-angels. Without risks, there are no rewards. It goes deeper than that, though; with no risks, we are doomed not to experience the learning, explore new relationships, or have the true delight of loving someone. When the time comes, we may not be able to open the door to let that right pre-angel in because we are so comfortable in our single lifestyle. We need to grow and learn from every relationship, and if we don't allow the man or woman into our world, then we will never know what other happiness the universe had in store for us.

The greatest fear for most, single pre-angels, is feeling lonely and dying alone. Understand that you are never alone for there are many spirits, guides and mentors with us from all levels of existence even if you cannot see them.

Song Reference:
All I Need is an Angel **by Rae Jepsen**

Affairs

An affair, from the deep side of understanding, means that a pre-angel is missing one or more of the seven senses in his/her life. It is actually about himself/herself, and not about the current relationship but when the current relationship is not fulfilling, many will mask it with an affair. They feel an affair will fill a void in their present relationship because they are unable to recognize the missing elements. They convince themselves that having an affair will satisfy their wants and fulfill the missing sense(s), for subconsciously pre-angels know which sense they are missing.

Affairs are logical approaches to dealing with the missing senses, so fulfilling "the wants" does not usually lead to a lasting relationship. Having an affair is an ego feeling, and is only temporary. There are different types of affairs, including making out, having sex and emotional affairs. Affairs start with a connection of the invisible vibrational energy that surrounds the couple. They discover this when they are talking or just staring at each other. It's not the physical and sexual attraction that brings them together; it is the invisible vibrational energy between the two. The invisible vibrational energy can result in an emotional connection, then the affair progresses and a sexual attraction follows.

Logical pre-angels have more affairs for quick fixes in their lives than deep sided pre-angels. The logical pre-angel feels more alive during the affair, but this is only temporary deepness. Temporary deepness fades away after the pre-angel is back to being him/herself. If the missing sense(s) are not fulfilled, then the affair will continue. After the missing sense(s) are recovered, the affair will slowly shift. It stays at one stage, becomes stale, or will end.

The sense(s) that the pre-angel are missing within him/herself and in the current relationship will determine the type of affair he/she is likely to have.

Invisible Vibrational Energy & Sight

The Technology Affair: When a pre-angel is chatting on the internet with someone other than his/her partner, discussing personal issues, their life story and expressing emotions about their current relationship. He/she is missing the emotional connection with their partner, and not hearing enough positive words on the home front. Communication is lacking in the present relationship, and the pre-angel is unable to identify what he/she wants and needs.

Hear

The Phone Sex Affair: The pre-angel is only hearing complaints in their current relationship and missing the positive words and appreciation that is needed to keep self-esteem at a high level. He/she would like to hear the soft tone, and experience the missing hearing elements. Words do hurt. Kind words work.

Touch & Smell & Taste

The Sexual Affair: This is when a pre-angel has a sexual affair focused on the want approach because he/she is missing touch, smell and taste which is a part of sex. Wants are temporary, resulting in a lack of sustainability of the affair and the rewards of sex, which are wants and from the logical side, will fade away over time. This type of affair is a result of lacking hugs, affectionate intimacies, and deepness in the areas of their life that bring the needs and wants together.

All Seven Senses

The Full Blown Affair: This is when a pre-angel is having an emotional and sexual affair. The couple is meeting secretly, having sex, sexting, and forming an emotional connection. The affair takes over their lives. This type of affair means that the individual is very lost. He/she is unhappy in all areas of his/her identity, job, children, and the current relationship. He/she has lost the ability to know who they are and do not know their needs and wants. This type of affair leads to a crisis of spirit and feeling that the whole world is coming down. The logical pre-angel will believe that sex is a deepness tool to recover from their identity crisis.

Affairs can be devastating to the partner who endures this hurtful betrayal. It is difficult to understand that the pre-angel who is having the affair is lost. When a pre-angel is confused and lost in the logical world, they won't act like themselves. This however, is not excuse but at least an understanding.

Can a relationship succeed after an affair? It depends on the relationship. Both partners can achieve peace by acknowledging the missing sense(s) within themselves and in the current relationship. If both want to continue in the relationship, they must trust and have forgiveness. Lack of trust is an obstacle for many that will cast a shadow on the relationship. Some say that once someone has had an affair, he/she will do so again and again. This can occur because the missing sense(s) is only being filled temporarily by the affair and will want to be fulfilled again. In this case, the pre-angel continues to have affairs.

The solution is for the individual to remove him/herself from all relationships and find out who they want to be. Focusing on the deep side therapies will be essential to finding out who they want to be now and identifying the missing senses. Traditional logical therapy will not achieve these results, as the affair is a logical solution, or rather just a quick fix. We need to resolve the crisis on the deep side, so deep side therapy will help with these missing sense(s).

Broken Hearts

The life you knew has been shattered like a broken mirror, and you can't see yourself in the mirror anymore. It's best to leave the mirror pieces alone instead of picking them up and hurting yourself again. A broken heart is like someone dying, grief, doubt, pain and anger all grouped into one feeling. A broken heart can blind us into believing that there are no more possibilities. It can rob us of joyful plans and make us question our memories. If you have never had a broken heart, take your index finger and press it into your chest where your heart is located. That's what a broken heart feels like, but the pressure is continuous, day and night. It's difficult to breathe. We must realize that many factors lead up to a broken heart. Perhaps the former partner was not your soul mate; maybe one of you grew, while the other stayed the same; perhaps there was unloving behavior or mental illness, etc. If we just go with the motions, we don't see the whole relationship that we are in until we step back and see who we have become. Sometimes we don't like ourselves anymore, and we don't know how we got to this point. A relationship is two pre-angels becoming one, but each is still an individual. So we must be careful not to lose that individuality in a relationship.

Your world is not falling apart,
it's falling right into place"
~ Fidgal

Whatever the cause, a broken heart feels like someone has died; grief takes over your heart. Your heart is broken, but it doesn't have to stop beating. In the beginning stages, you are shattered and a rush of emotions come full force. The relationship you had yesterday is now closed. You feel that the current chapter in your life is over; it doesn't mean that you can't pick up the pieces and start a new journey. This new journey will take time, and it will appear when you are ready. Sometimes the universe has another man or woman waiting for you but you have to let go of your broken heart to see it.

Divorce

Shattered by what you thought your life was going to be, you wonder where you will go from here.

No one can control anyone in a relationship. One of the hardest life events to go through is a divorce, even if it is for a good reason. The love that you shared has faded away and you are unable to capture the same invisible vibrational energy that you had at the beginning. This is the ultimate rejection, a feeling of failure that leads to fear. Fear is an illusion of the unknown. The routine of family life, the traditions and notions that in our mind gave us comfort has been removed. The memories that were shared feel empty and unreal. We analyze and reanalyze what went wrong, are not able to sleep and have an empty heart. We'll question ourselves constantly. How did I get to this point? Was the relationship real or fake? Voices play in our heads, and in our hearts. Divorce is a learning process of understanding how a couple got to a separation in their lives.

<u>To understand divorce from a deep side is simple: a long-term relationship was not meant to be</u>. Divorce does not mean that you will never find your soul mate; it means that you are more likely to find your soul mate. That understanding doesn't take away the hurt. Divorce includes grief and numerous other emotions being played in our hearts and replaying in our minds. Divorce is a logical solution that affects the deep side and is all wrapped up into one feeling - failure. Did you fail? You might feel that you failed, but to the universe it was not meant to be and a new chapter is being created.

Feelings of failure creep up especially when children are involved. We may feel like failures because we did not hold the family together. Many parents have an attachment to showing their children that they know everything and can accomplish everything. When a divorce occurs, the attachment to knowing everything is gone in the eyes of the children. Parents need to understand that they teach their children about life but their children teach them about living. Let go of the notion that we won't make any mistakes, and instead show their children that it's ok to let go.

Understanding the reason why you're getting divorced is critical. It helps couples to heal. Often it's because the invisible vibrational energy has faded away, creating a ripple effect to other areas in the relationship including love, sex, intimacy, and communication. There can be any number of reasons why pre-angels get divorced.

When the couple cannot get back the love, they try to replace it with the material possessions. The material possessions will not mask the hurt that they feel. These possessions do not heal the deep side. That's why divorce is so difficult to process. We are compensating for the deep side with logical side, and it doesn't fulfill the hurt and pain that we are going through in our hearts. We take care of the logical material possessions first and then we can heal the deep side. The deep side will take longer to heal, as it is the deep side that has been damaged and hurt. We have to do more deep side therapies to get through this difficult time. From the previous chapter, we identified needs as long-term sustainability and wants as the logical side, so the logical side is faster to take care of than the deep side.

Divorce is a logical resolution to a separation. When lawyers get involved, we will receive logical results. Involving a spiritual mentor (deep sided) along with a lawyer (logical) will provide more balanced, peaceful results. It sounds very odd, but divorces do not have to be negative. If the ego lets go of money and material possessions, divorces can be peaceful. When both parties attack each other in court, they are affecting the deep side more than the logical side. When pre-angels can't get the love back they will feel the need to use anger to get the material possessions and money. The energy and the hurt feelings are all coming from the deep side. The peaceful goal of divorce is for the ex-partner to become a friend down the road. When you can become their friend, then you have achieved the letting go and forgiveness.

Unable to Let Go

No regrets! No one wants regrets, so many couples will try the *"last hope of reconciling"* the relationship one last time. They see a traditional counselor, maybe take a stress leave from work and even try sleeping in separate bedrooms in the same house to see if the passion will return. Many couples keep trying and trying for some time. At some point, they may start changing themselves for the other spouse just to get along. At a point in the relationship they know exactly where they have to go: either salvage the marriage by being someone else or end it.

When you have to change for someone else, it doesn't last. In the beginning it will work, but later pre-angels will return to being themselves. They cannot continue the act, and do what they want too. Who wants to act all the time? That's not loving yourself and being honest with who you are. You live in the same house, but feel like a stranger living there. Einstein explained that when we surround ourselves with a lower energy, we get pulled down to that energy level. It becomes difficult to keep the invisible vibration energy to our level. This logical behavior will continue until someone gets tired enough to call it quits. Calling it quits doesn't mean failure, it means freedom. We should have freedom to find out who we want to be now and release all the painful memories and empty promises that have hurt us. *Sometimes holding on does more damage than letting go.*

The traditional counselor is great from a logical side, and some couples may be successful using this treatment, but love resonates on our deep side as it connects to emotions, and has nothing to do with the logical side. Therefore, going to a traditional counselor will result in logical answers, but will not give the couple the direction they need to maintain their relationship. What they need is to find themselves individually. The best way is giving each other space, sometimes known as pulling away. Male pre-angels are known to do this more than female's pre-angels. Giving each other space is a good way to allow time to think, process feelings and figure out what is wanted and needed in the relationship. Unfortunately, when pre-angels pull away they do not communicate that they need space, and it leaves some pre-angels impatient. Once you have pulled away, it's necessary to regroup and present what you have discovered and what you want to say to your spouse and do going forward. Taking space to think is a good way of loving yourself. We all need space, and finding ourselves will help us understand what we want and need.

Too much emphasis is put on traditional therapy (counseling) to resolve relationship matters. A life coach and/or a spiritual mentor should be incorporated into the process as well. These are the therapies that will help you to find out who you want to be now and achieve balance in your life. Many traditional counselors advise couples to take a trip to see if the flame will rekindle. This is great but when you return reality hits again and usually the flame won't last. A trip provides a change of environment. When you return home, it's back to the familiar, the same old everyday problems. Also many traditional therapists will advise the couple to stay in the relationship up to one year and see if it will work. As explained in the divorce section, if you have to act or be something you are not, it's not worth it. These are surface behaviors and it's only temporary. One can only act for a certain amount of time until blowing up from holding everything in. A balance of traditional therapy (logical) and life coaching or spiritual mentor (deep) is needed, with a bit more deep, for as the teachings say: slightly lead with your heart. Explore more of the deep side to resolve problems within. You can continue to try one last time, but if you continue to do everything and get the same results, then it's time to move on and get a divorce.

"It can be scary to trust the unknown"
~ Fidgal

It's time to separate from your past to move forward with your future. Untangle your past and get things done in the present. It is important to reset and go back to loving yourself using deep side therapies. Getting a divorce is moving on to another chapter in your life. It's time to take a different path. The scary part is the unknown. If we trust the universe and love ourselves, then we will make better decisions that will lead us to happiness.

Song Reference:
***Tell Your Heart to Beat Again* by Danny Gokey**

CHAPTER 7

Unconditional Love

"To love yourself is the ultimate gift of love"
~ Fidgal

Forgiveness

JESUS EXPLAINED THAT FORGIVENESS will set us free and that we need to forgive in order to move on to another chapter in our lives. The strength of forgiveness comes from the heart, and the not forgiving comes from the ego. When we forgive, we boost the invisible vibrational energy around us. In this chapter, we will explore how forgiveness can heal the soul and spirit.

The key to unlocking the door, to bringing back love, peace and balance is forgiveness. It's the toughest thing to do and usually the last thing on your mind. Forgiveness is the ultimate way of letting go of someone who betrayed you.

When we do not forgive, we hold it in our heart. Blood travels through our hearts and if we hold negative energy in our hearts then all the blood that travels through it will become tainted. It's like a poison going through our organs and everywhere that the blood moves. Many diseases and mental illnesses can occur in our body because we cannot forgive. The universe forgives us all the time, so if the highest source can forgive why can't we?

We enable the ego to take over our lives. We hear accusing voices that don't allow us to forgive ourselves and others. This is the voice of the ego. Forgiveness saves the one that is closest to your hearts, and that is you! When you cannot forgive, you are the problem standing in the way of total freedom. Attaching yourselves to anger, hurt and other negative invisible vibrational energies can ruin your life. To forgive is freeing your soul from being a prisoner and allowing more positivity to come into your life. You sometimes make wrong turns, but that does not stop your destiny. A choice was presented, and you decided to take the detour, but that doesn't mean you have to stay on that road. Pre-angels that have done you harm can put you at a disadvantage, but you have the choice to give them the power to continue to do so. Remember a great mess can become greatness. <u>It is important to forgive ourselves first and take responsibility for our actions then we can forgive others</u>.

The pain of betrayal is only the original blow. The trauma witnessed or experienced lives on in our memories. Wrongful revenge causes unfairness through outrage in our heart. Anger and bitterness do not poison us alone. They poison all the relationships that are similar to what we experienced.

"Those who are preparing for revenge are really seeking inner peace that will never be found"
~ Fidgal

It is normal to want to get back at someone who did wrong to you. But hurting someone just satisfies the ego, not the heart. To experience healing and deepness is to forgive. Not forgiving can cause depression and loss of hope, mental illness, health problems, increase anger inside and disconnection of self. Hanging on to something from the past that you cannot fix is like driving in reverse and not getting anywhere. To forgive is to lead with the heart and let go, and is to be part of the solution.

Song Reference:
***Forgiveness* by Matthew West**

Teaching Ten

It is important to reflect that we create our own nightmares by not forgiving. Forgiveness is a deep side action and it represents how we feel about ourselves. To forgive is the greatest strength, the greatest kindness in our hearts. Let go of what was suppose to be a learning experience but has developed into a prison sentence. To love ourselves is to let go of pre-angels who have done us wrong.

Law of Attraction

If it's not meant to be, the universe will keep giving us the same results no matter how many times you try. The **Law of Attraction** is the science of attracting what we want/need in our lives, our thoughts and feelings manifesting at universal pace. The universe continuously shows us what the universe wants us to know by giving messages. When this occurs, we need to recognize, understand and embrace this. The universe doesn't just examine our thoughts and feelings, but also the energy that we put out there. Whatever we put out we will get back. The universe knows us better than we know ourselves and puts pre-angels, resources and situations in our life. Many pre-angels are misusing the law of attraction and focusing only on their wants. The focus must be on what we "need" in our lives to sustain us. It's fine to use the law of attraction in all areas of our lives involving both wants and needs, but know that the needs are more sustainable than the wants. Focus on the needs and trust the process that the universe will provide for us. To love ourselves is to focus on what the universe keeps showing. If we continually get the same unsatisfactory or uncomfortable results, it is time to take a different road.

The negative side of the law of attraction is that the universe will match our thoughts, feelings and invisible vibrational energy. When we focus on negative things, we will receive them. The best way to manifest is to request something positive, think positive thoughts and always lead with your heart.

Picture This

A hockey player who wants to win the state championship uses law of attraction. He convinces himself and
his father that with hard work and dedication he will
achieve the goal of winning the state championship. But
is that what he wants? Does he want the championship
or the feeling that is locked into winning the championship? We may want to win, but the universe knows what
we feel and need. In this case, the championship is
what he wants, what he needs is the feeling of achieve-
ment, of being looked up to and honored. The universe
knows our feelings and is always willing to help out with
what we are missing in our lives. In this case, the
hockey player needed to belong to a team and wanted
that feeling of belonging. He also wanted to spend time
with his father and needed to be seen by him. Even if
we don't know what we want or need, the universe does
know and will provide it. There is always a reason for
everything. With anything that we would like to manifest,
we must help the universe by taking the necessary actions to complete it. He wanted to be a champion, so he
attended hockey practice and learned how to skate
faster, etc. We have to show the universe that we are
on board with everything and help with the manifesting.

We cannot lie to the universe, even if we want something badly and do everything to get it. The universe
knows exactly what we need at different times in our
lives. At times, we are so focused on what we want that
we do not see what is in front of us. The golden ticket at
times is staring us in the face. We may just not see it

because we are so focused on other things that we want to manifest.

Oftentimes, we will continue fighting for a certain result, but if it doesn't happen the universe is teaching us to let it go and aim for something different. Holding on or fighting for what we believe is a great motivation, but when we do not get the happy results and continue to force the manifesting we tend to get the same results. We sabotage our lives with holding on to the belief and forcing the manifesting. When one fights for something they believe in and it starts taking over their life, then it's not meant to be. The universe is teaching us to let go and allow the universe to lead.

"Our lives are changing, and we have to
catch up to what the universe wants us to change"
~ Fidgal

Love Yourself

Out of all the teachings that Einstein and Jesus taught me, this by far is the most powerful teaching of all. By loving ourselves we show the universe that we are ready for the next chapter in our lives. Jesus and Einstein both believed that the truth about our lives lies within the love for ourselves.

We are the hardest pre-angels on ourselves. We will often blame ourselves a thousand times for the same mistake, instead of loving ourselves unconditionally. How do we love ourselves unconditionally? We need to spend time with ourselves. This is called "Me Time," which is essential to getting to know ourselves. It is important that we understand me time. **Me time** is a time when we do something alone that increases awareness of who we are and gives us happiness. For example, we could go to the spa or take ourselves out to a movie. Spending time with you is part of the process of growing. When we know who we are, we can see our limitations and apply them to our life so we won't get hurt. Everyone should take two hours per week from their busy schedule and do something just for himself or herself. Uncontrollable events that we will not love will happen in our lives, but if we accept them it will be easier to love ourselves.

We must take time to obtain self-awareness to better ourselves using the deep side therapies and activities. Self-awareness requires taking the time to get to know who you are by doing me time, reading self-help books, and attending a retreat, etc. These are a few of the deep side therapies and exercises that can enhance your self-awareness. (See the end of chapter 1 for more deep side therapies and exercises). If we continually work on self-awareness we will not become lost at times of crisis. We won't have to start at the beginning or be emotionally scarred forever.

When we do not get results we want, we often start doubting ourselves or feel like we don't deserve what we want. To love ourselves is to trust that the universe will provide everything in time. Be grateful for what you do have, and know that you deserve it.

Sometimes pre-angels believe they are giving unconditional love but then start making comments and giving directions to pre-angels. When this occurs the ego has crept up and taken over. This is conditional love with limits and is not genuine. Unconditional love has no limitations. We must learn to accept pre-angels and ourselves with unconditional love.

To love yourself is to love everything about you and apply it to the Mind, Body, Heart, Spirit and Soul that make up the unique you. Here are some suggestions to assist you with loving yourself.

Body

Eat healthy foods that are natural to maintain a healthy weight and feel good from the inside out. Always use a gentle touch. Treat yourself with something that gives you pleasure in moderation.

Mind

Only think and say positive words, and imagine positive things. Meditate to find peace in your wandering minds. Be open to everything in existence.

Heart

Give and allow others to give to you, as receiving is part of the heart. Act using your heart. Send love to the pre-angels who have done you wrong.

Spirit

Be true to who you are. Be natural. The universe made you in a certain way; never change for someone. Accept others for who they are and embrace them into your life. Learn from them.

Soul

Always be loving to your soul. Be kind. Explore your passion. Most of all live in the moment. Use logical and deep side therapies to maintain balance and a peaceful life.

It is important to know that divine time will happen when the universe feels it is necessary; it usually occurs when we are balanced in a certain area of our lives. We cannot control all areas of our lives, but the one thing that we can control is the feelings about ourselves. Loving ourselves is giving unconditional love to our soul, body, spirit, mind and heart. The key to succeed in this world is finding inner peace, and loving ourselves is the primary way of achieving this. Show the universe that you do deserve inner peace; take what the universe is giving, and go for it. BELIEVE.

Teaching Eleven

The key to maintaining balance is to continue to love ourselves unconditionally and keep going when times are rough and uncertain. Remove the ego and know that the universe made you perfect and trusted you with a certain purpose. Take 'me time' and get to know who you are and continue incorporating self-awareness into your lifestyle.

Some More About Me

Many have asked if I forgive the counselor. I will be honest here. It is hard to forgive someone who has never acknowledged what she has done. I accept though, that if the universe did not want me to go through this, then the universe would have changed it. I hope that she learned from the experience, became peaceful with what occurred and that she became a better counselor. Hopefully, at some point the counselor will be brave enough to discuss with me what occurred and her intentions. It is my wish that one day she will apologize for being so unaware. At times, I do believe that she was trying to protect me and was put in a delicate situation. The words that she spoke way back then altered my life forever. She applied her beliefs and assumptions to this type of situation and it created many obstacles in my life including in the education system and my personal life. Without her doing this I would have never learned the true meaning of forgiveness and letting go.

I am happy that I had to go through this heart problem when I was so young. I don't even remember the pain or the hospital days. Sometimes going through a health crisis at an early age is better than at an older age when you will remember the pain.

Throughout my journey in heaven and living here, I have learned to understand that everything happens exactly the way it was meant to be, and that I would not change anything.

> *"If we change anything,*
> *It would change everything"*
> *~ Fidgal*

The health problems that I endured gave me the ability to be sympathetic towards others that are dealing with conditions. We all are going to face health and other problems, but if we apply the deep and logical side to treating them, they will subside. I wouldn't change my journey; it has made me who I am today. I am perfect in my own way! Because I have balance, I often feel that my medical problems don't exist. I live a good life, a life that the universe has created for me.

For a long time I really didn't live my life to the fullest because I suppressed so many memories of heaven. Now I try everything. My family and friends say that I have so much energy and get involved with too many activities. After something like freedom is taken from you, you fly with it when you get it back.

Throughout the years, I have learned and accepted that no one is responsible for my feelings and emotions and I have come to peace with telling my story to everyone, no matter the outcome. My story was hidden, but the journey the universe wants for me, is just starting. And, hopefully, it's starting for you too.

Song Reference:
Don't Stop Believin' by Journey

Teaching Twelve

The last and most profound teaching, is to never lose sight of who you are and don't worry what pre-angels think of you. Be honest with yourself and be yourself. The older we get the more we will realize that we don't care about what pre-angels think.

SUMMARY OF TEACHINGS:
HOW TO ACHIEVE BALANCE
AND FIND PEACE WITHIN

Teaching One

It is important to note that our hearts are slightly to the left of our chests; therefore we should lead slightly with our heart (55%) when making decisions and living life. We should incorporate deep sided therapies & exercises into our lifestyle to achieve this balance which in the end will grant us peace.

Teaching Two

The logical side does have to be recognized temporarily and let go. We should allow the logical side to follow using 45%. If one attaches too much to the logical side, then illusion will take over. We need both the logical and deep sides to balance and find peace, for using only one will not maintain life.

Teaching Three

It is important to understand when someone is leading too much either with the logical or deep side then a crisis of spirit, also known as an identity crisis will occur. Furthermore, we must seek professional help using both types of treatment (logical, deep) to achieve balance again. To resolve this type of crisis we must incorporate the therapies and exercises from the opposite side of that which is leading with the 80%. We must reset ourselves to become aware of living in the now.

Teaching Four

If everyone learned about detachment then we would not have any problems in this world, in this current life or when we return. Detachment is the skill of letting go of anything that is holding us back from achieving our purpose and being who we want to be. Once we detach, we will become balanced again. Detachment is a healthy way of living and must be done throughout our lives to maintain a healthy spirit, mind, body, heart and soul.

Teaching Five

Destiny's time not our time! We need patience to believe in the universe by choosing the right course of free will. We do not have to understand it; we just need to follow through with what the universe is giving us. Messages are guiding us to achieve. At times though, we mess it up by choosing a different path. The universe, however, will continue to give us the same message until we act on it.

Teaching Six

Invisible Vibrational Energy is the most profound sense that is overlooked and not even acknowledged. This invisible feeling of energy is also called "intuitive energy." It builds up our trust factor and is always around us. We should trust our intuition.

Teaching Seven

It is critical to understand that we are never alone in this world. No one will succeed without others, plus, we always have the universe helping us to achieve greatness. We are not alone, and should work as a team to resolve issues and to achieve our purpose. We need to remove the competitiveness as there is enough to go around.

Teaching Eight

In any relationship we have, communication is primary. So many times couples break up because one is not honest with themselves or their partner. Truth is harder than a lie and we forget the lie at times. To understand anyone, we must be honest. When you are honest and communicate that way, it will set you free. No one knows what you are thinking.

Teaching Nine

When something in our lives is rough and unpleasant, we must learn from it and let it go. Holding on to someone who is not allowing growth is holding us back from the next chapter in our lives that the universe has set up. To let go is the hardest thing to do, but the strongest way that you can show love for yourself.

Teaching Ten

It is important to reflect that we create our own nightmares by not forgiving. Forgiveness is a deep side action and it represents how we feel about ourselves. To forgive is the greatest strength, the greatest kindness in our hearts. Let go of what was supposed to be a learning experience but has developed into a prison sentence. To love ourselves is to let go of pre-angels who have done us wrong.

Teaching Eleven

The key to maintaining balance is to continue to love ourselves unconditionally and keep going when times are rough and uncertain. Remove the ego and know that the universe made you perfect and trusted you with a certain purpose. Take 'me time' and get to know who you are and continue incorporating self-awareness into your lifestyle.

Teaching Twelve

The last and most profound teaching, is to never lose sight of who you are and don't worry what pre-angels think of you. Be honest with yourself and be yourself. The older we get the more we will realize that we don't care about what pre-angels think.

Song References

Palmer. F, (1981), Morning train [Recorded by Sheena Easton] *Sheena Easton* [CD], EMI American

Bourgeois, Brent. Tumes, Michelle. (2006). I will rest in you [Recorded by Jaci Velasquez]. *On My Knees – The Best of Jaci Velasquez* [CD], World Entertainment LLC.

B. Morris, Antonoff. J, Williams, J. Levine, J. Platten. R, (2015). Stand by you [Recorded by Rachel Platten]. *Wildfire* [CD]. Columbia

Moccio. S, Masri. M, Ryan, Kowarsky. D, Kowarsky, R, (2006). The face [Recorded by RayDan]. *RyanDan* [CD]. Universal Music.

Foreman. J, (2007) This is your life [Recorded by Switchfoot]. *The Beautiful Letdown* [CD] Columbia.

Larsson. M, Frediksson. R, Holter. O, Michaels, Julia & Tranter J, (2014). Love myself [Recorded by Hailee Steinfeld] [CD]. *Love Myself*. Republic Records

Rinehart. N, Rinehart. W, (2012) Keep your eyes open. [Recorded by Need to Breath [CD]. *Reckoning*, Atlantic

Kasher. J, Hindlin. J, Dobson. F, Rudolf. K, Dioguardi. K. (2010) Ghost [Recorded by Fefe Dobson] [CD], *Joy*, Island

DeGarmo, D, Young. A, (2011) Good Goodbye (2011) [Recorded by Diana De Garmo] [CD]. *Good Goodbye - Single*, Mailboat Records.

Chrisman. A, Kenney J., Krippayne S, (2011) Atmosphere [Recorded by Andy Chrisman] [CD]. *One.* Catapult.

Kitt T, Yorkey B., (2016) All I need is an angel [Recorded by Carly Rae Jepsen] [CD] *Grease Live!" Music From The Television Event,* Paramount/Republic Record

Herms, B., West M., Phillips R, (2014) Tell your heart to beat again [Recorded by Danny Gokey] [CD] *Hope in Front of Me.* BMG Rights Management

West. M,. (2012) Forgiveness [Recorded by Matthew West] [CD] *Into the Light.* Sparrow Records

Cain. J, Schon N., Perry. S, (1981) Don't Stop Believin' [Recorded by Journey] [CD] *Escape,* Song BMG Music Entertainment

Acknowledgments

This book exists thanks to the sunshine and the influence of so many pre-angels that I have come across in my life time, in this world and on the other side.

Jesus & Albert Einstein – Thank you for passing on your knowledge and for choosing me to deliver it, I have been forever blessed. The essence of their messages has inspired me to write this book and share their voices with the world.

Eugenio Iuliano (Nonno) - To the greatest story teller of all, my grandfather. Even though we live far away, you have given me the ability to tell a story in a funny but logical way. Thank you!

Elisa Iuliano (Mom) – My first and greatest teacher, you taught me not to listen to negative words and always to think positive. You were always at my bedside worrying about me in the hospital, and I truly appreciate your unconditional love. You are a mother who has endured so much over the years with my health but has still managed to stay positive and optimistic. I love you and thank you!

Giuseppe Iuliano (Dad) – A man of strength and an incredible heart. I have been truly blessed when you held me in your hand. You have been a wonderful provider, and I am proud to call you my father. I love you always and thank you!

Gino Iuliano (Brother) – To a man who has taught me more about living than anyone on earth. Each day is an adventure with you and I thank you for making these days so interesting!

Meeka (Niece) – To a beautiful, cute little girl who has given me a glimpse of who I use to be as a child. Your kind heart and contagious smile have given me the ultimate gift of love. Thank you for always being happy and for all your hugs!

Heidi McLarty – One of my soul sisters and a great light in my world. You have given me the joy of experiencing life with Fidgal and accepting us unconditionally. I look forward to more adventures to come with you. Thank you for supporting me with all our craziness and my new ideas.

Leslie Dafoe – So many of the beautiful actions that a friend can give have come from you. Thank you for believing in me and for always taking the time during your busy life to spend a little time with me.

Dawna Kinnunen – You have been one of the most influential pre-angels in my life. Thank you for teaching me to have faith in myself and helping me to find the courage to change my career to better my life.

Steven Shoemaker – You are more than my cousin, you are a valued friend. You are always in the shadows, always willing to view any documents. I thank you for being real and always protecting me.

Andrea Reibmayr & Dr. Elder – I thank you for allowing me to write this amazing book at your beautiful cabin. The joy that surrounds your family is a true blessing.

Sandra Hodge - I am forever grateful for that you took the time to help me with understanding the language of literature; you are one of the wisest of all. You accept everyone including myself for who they are and I thank you for being an angel and surrounding me with your positive energy.

Brenda Eagle-Ransom – You have been part of this book's journey from day one. It's always a pleasure being around you. Your interest and encouragement in my book has given me the power and motivation to complete it. Thank you for always sending me love and positive energy.

Brenda Swystun – You are a strong and fearless woman, and I have enjoyed bouncing various deep sided information off you. Thank you for your logical sided view.

Cynthia (Cindy) Clement – Thank you for always being there, whether I had a short question or a long story to tell. You are an amazing woman who has taught me so much about being an author. Thank you for being who you are!

John Clement – For believing in the power of my story from the start and giving me messages to help me along in my path of life. Thank you for being a great teacher and a fantastic mentor. You are always in my heart.

Dr. Wayne Dyer – To a man that I never met in the human form but affected my heart with your words of power in so many books. Your knowledge and powerful influence have given me the courage to write this book. See you at the gate!

Shelley Wright – To a wise woman, who has taught me a lot about the life and always being real. Thank you for being such a great friend and supporting me.

Bruce Cave – Your faith and commitment to understanding my story has given me the greatest gift, the ability to be a great teacher and a humble student. You have taught me that anyone can make a change; you only need hope and God. Thank you for being a great friend and amazing teacher.

Professor Vincent D'Agostino – A teacher who has impacted the lives of so many students. You light the way for so many pre-angels. Thank you for sharing all your stories and knowledge of the peace world. You have opened my eyes to a whole new world of love and peace.

Darren Edmond – To an amazingly talented artist and friend. We can agree to disagree with each other and still have a good laugh. Thank you for creating an amazing Fidgal logo.

Robert Hanson – The message that you gave me was so profound that it shifted my consciousness and has made me who I am today. You were my life changer. Thank you for being at the right place at the right time.

Gail Nelson – To a wonderful, kind person who gives help to others and asks for nothing in return. Thank you for helping me with this book.

Mark Primavera (Photographer) – What gifts you give to the photographer world! You make me look amazing in those pictures. Your kindness and talent will not go unrecognized. Thank you for sharing your gifts.

Katie Alton (Graphic Artist) – To a talented graphic artist who has shown the world the images in my mind. Your commitment and service have been a wonderful gift in my life. Thank you for helping me to create my vision and for listening to my stories while we draw.

Linda Zeppa (Editor) – To my talented editor, your commitment to helping me tell my story has given me the greatest gift of all – HOPE. You make my book look like a masterpiece, a work of art filled with empowering messages using your gift of language. I thank you and will always remember our time together writing this book especially the peach and ginger pop. ☺

To all my aunts, uncles and lots of cousins: Each of you brings sunshine into my world with your presence and your endless interest in my stories and adventures. So many happy memories are tied into my life with all of you. I thank you for always supporting me in all I do.

To all the amazing pre-angels who have influenced my life through their gift of singing and composing music that I have referenced in this book. You inspire many, the joy; the emotional and positive energy that you have placed into these songs does change this world! Throughout my life, I have met so many pre-angels along the way, and I thank you for sharing your stories with me. Thank you for taking the time to listen to my story and encouraging me to write this book.

Fidgal – Thank you for being my guardian angel and guiding me here on earth and in heaven. I am forever grateful for the role that you play in my life. You are one of my favorite spirits! I trust you with all my heart. I love you! ☺

About the Author

My real name is Maria Iuliano, and at the age five years old, I had a near-death experience. While I was in heaven, I met my Guardian Angel named Fidgal. So I took his name as my pen name! :)

Next upcoming book

"Direct Every Angel to Heaven"

Discover the truth about who you are and where you are going. Learn the different dimensions in heaven.
Available January 2017.

Contact Information

Visit our web site: **www.fidgal.com**

E-MAIL: **fidgal@fidgal.com**

Like Us Facebook: **Fidgal**

Instagram: **Fidgaltheauthor**

Twitter: **@Fidgal**

Made in the USA
Columbia, SC
24 May 2017